Karen J. Miller, Ph.D., is a clinical neuropsychologist at the University of California, Los Angeles, Medical Center. Her clinical and research career has focused on the effects of hormones on cognition and mood, early detection of Alzheimer's Disease, and memory enhancement for age-related memory decline. She is also director of the Neuropsychology Externship Training Program at UCLA, where she trains graduate students in cognitive assessment. She is the author of numerous abstracts and scientific journal articles, presents at national and international conferences, and conducts continuing education seminars for professionals.

Steven A. Rogers, Ph.D., is assistant professor of clinical psychology at Westmont College in Santa Barbara, CA. His clinical and research career has focused on the neuropsychology of dementia and disorders of aging, the effects of hormones on mood, and the early detection of Alzheimer's disease. He is the author of numerous abstracts and scientific journal articles, presents at national and international conferences, and also provides psychotherapy in private practice.

Foreword writer Gary Small, MD, is professor of psychiatry and biobehavioral sciences at the University of California, Los Angeles.

D0958239

THE ESTROGEN-DEPRESSION CONNECTION

The Hidden Link Between Hormones & Women's Depression

KAREN J. MILLER, PH.D.
STEVEN A. ROGERS, PH.D.

New Harbinger Publications, Inc.

Publisher's Note

Care has been taken to confirm the accuracy of the information presented and to describe generally accepted practices. However, the authors, editors, and publisher are not responsible for errors or omissions or for any consequences from application of the information in this book and make no warranty, express or implied, with respect to the contents of the publication.

The authors, editors, and publisher have exerted every effort to ensure that any drug selection and dosage set forth in this text are in accordance with current recommendations and practice at the time of publication. However, in view of ongoing research, changes in government regulations, and the constant flow of information relating to drug therapy and drug reactions, the reader is urged to check the package insert for each drug for any change in indications and dosage and for added warnings and precautions. This is particularly important when the recommended agent is a new or infrequently employed drug.

Some drugs and medical devices presented in this publication may have Food and Drug Administration (FDA) clearance for limited use in restricted research settings. It is the responsibility of the health care provider to ascertain the FDA status of each drug or device planned for use in their clinical practice.

Distributed in Canada by Raincoast Books

Copyright © 2007 by Karen Miller and Steven Rogers
New Harbinger Publications, Inc.
5674 Shattuck Avenue
Oakland, CA 94609
www.newharbinger.com

Cover and text design by Amy Shoup; Acquired by Melissa Kirk; Edited by Elisabeth Beller

---

Library of Congress Cataloging-in-Publication Data

Miller, Karen J.
  The estrogen-depression connection : the hidden link between hormones and women's depression /
Karen J. Miller and Steven A. Rogers.
    p. cm.
  ISBN-13: 978-1-57224-483-2
  ISBN-10: 1-57224-483-6
  1. Menopause--Hormone therapy--Complications. 2. Estrogen--Physiological effect. I. Rogers, Steven
A. II. Title.
  RG186.E8893 2007
  618.1'75061--dc22

                                  2007005747

09   08   07

10   9   8   7   6   5   4   3   2   1

First printing

Table of Contents

What Is Estrogen? • Estrogen & Early Brain Organization • Estrogen
& the Brain After Birth • Other Biochemical Effects of Estrogen •
Circadian Rhythms • Estrogen & Men • Conclusion

The Sad Truth • Puberty & the Emergence of Depression • Why the
Rise in Depression in Women? • The Face of Adolescent Depression •
Conclusion

Acknowledgments

First, I would like to thank Dr. Gary Small and Dr. Susan Bookheimer for countless opportunities to explore and expand my career in neuroscience. Their mentorship and modeling inspires me daily to be a better neuropsychologist. I am also thankful to Drs. Jarvik, Rasgon, and Bauer for the introduction into the world of hormones and their impact on the brain. My passion has been born, fueled, and inspired by these psychiatrists. Next I am thankful for my eighth-floor family at UCLA: Andrea, Debby, Linda, Prabha, Gwen, Tree, and Pauline, who have provided moral support over the years and countless stories about the impact of estrogen on real women. I am grateful to Dr. Jeanne Kim and her assistance with the reference list for this book. I am eternally thankful for the support and inspiration of my friends, clients, graduate students, and my family, especially John, Jean, and Jack, who have forgone many lazy Sundays in order for me to accomplish my career goals. Finally, I am most appreciative of my coauthor Dr. Steve Rogers, who has proven to be my dearest colleague and friend in this book-writing journey.

—Karen J. Miller, Ph.D.

The heart and soul of this book comes from my experience with female patients who have been gracious enough to share their stories and whose honesty has taught me more about estrogen and depression than I could learn from a textbook. They have helped me bridge the gender gap in ways I could not have imagined. I am deeply indebted to Dr. Nancy Vogt for teaching me what it means to truly listen, for helping me understand that theory is less important than presence, and for helping me to take what is fragmented in others and make it whole. I am deeply appreciative of Dr. Po Lu, who graciously provided space and encouragement for me to work on this project, despite needing help on several of his own. He has also provided unquestioning support and taught me a more holistic view of the person, where biology cannot be separated from psychology. I cannot thank my mom, nor my wife, Christina, enough for their love and sacrifice. My wife's patience and encouragement is the stuff of fairy tales, and so much of her own blood and sweat has been mixed into my career that it has become truly impossible to differentiate her effort from mine. And most of all, I want to thank my amazing coauthor, Dr. Karen Miller. She is a supervisor who became a mentor who became one of my closest friends. She has shaped my life in ways she could never fully appreciate, and there is no one else I would want to share this journey with. For that, and for her, I am eternally grateful.

—Steven A. Rogers, Ph.D.

Foreword

Thanks to advances in medical technology, women are living longer than ever before in history. And with this increase in life expectancy comes a longer time period during which the average woman will live in an estrogen-deficient state.

The growing interest in the mental effects of estrogen probably stems in part from the increased number of postmenopausal women in our aging society. Emerging scientific evidence (Kawas et al. 1997; Small 1998) from basic laboratory research, epidemiologic studies, and clinical trials is beginning to clarify the interaction between brain estrogen and mental states, and the millions of postmenopausal women who must face decisions about their choices regarding estrogen exposure will benefit from this information.

In this volume, Drs. Miller and Rogers provide a much-needed account of one of the most interesting aspects of these interactions—the connection between estrogen and depression. Their approach offers a cutting-edge perspective on what we know and don't know and translates the science into prose that will be accessible to a wide audience eager for accurate information.

Of course, any discussion of mood and aging also requires attention to cognition. As people age, they face an increased risk for memory loss and a variety of forms of cognitive impairment. Approximately 10 percent of women aged sixty-five and above experience cognitive decline that interferes with daily functioning (Small 2002). To complicate matters, older depressed women frequently complain about poor concentration, so clinicians often have difficulty differentiating a primary mood disorder from a cognitive one in late life.

Estrogen may mediate cognitive changes associated with aging. Studies of brain structures involved in memory show that estrogen facilitates the memory process by promoting better brain cell (neuron) activity. This promotion occurs because estrogen increases the communication between neurons, which is called *long-term potentiation* and *neuronal transmission*. Estrogen also improves the overall efficiency of the brain by augmenting cerebral blood flow and metabolism, as well as promoting cholinergic neurons. All of these are critical to normal cognitive functioning and have been observed to decline in people with dementia, suggesting that estrogen might be important in protecting the brain. Estrogen may also have an important impact on a person's brain and overall health because it modulates inflammation, genetics (apolipoprotein E), and the metabolism of the amyloid precursor protein, all of which influence cognitive functioning. Although some epidemiological studies have suggested that estrogen supplementation might protect a woman from Alzheimer's disease, clinical trials have not substantiated this link as yet.

A variety of mechanisms may also explain estrogen effects on mood (Schneider et al. 1997). Estrogen decreases certain receptors, increases specific hormones and neurotransmitters, and inhibits the enzyme monoamine oxidase (MAO-B), all of which have an impact on cognitive functions and mood. Specifically, in later life, depression is characterized by elevated levels of the enzyme MAO-B. High levels of MAO-B may result in less effective communication between brain cells as well as cell death due to *neurotoxins*.

Our research group has conducted several studies in attempts to further elucidate this potential estrogen-depression connection. The impact of estrogen therapy combined with antidepressants is of particular interest. In our study (Schneider et al. 1997) we looked at improvement of mood in a group of older depressed women that was given either a combined treatment of estrogen replacement therapy (ERT) and an antidepressant (fluoxetine) or a placebo (sugar pill, no active treatment). The women in the combined treatment improved significantly in their depression ratings when compared with those who were not taking the combination. In a second study of older depressed women (Schneider, Small, and Clary 2001), those taking both ERT and an antidepressant (sertraline) were found to have significantly greater global improvement and quality of life than those not receiving ERT. These same women also showed some improvement in anxiety and cognitive functioning. Since the potential estrogen interaction in these studies was determined after the fact, these studies warrant additional research that prospectively determines the influence of estrogen in depression treatment. However, they do support the hypothesis that ERT use without progesterone in older depressed women may augment antidepressant response.

While awaiting results from future studies, including the role of ERT for the treatment of depression in all phases of life, the current volume offers readers the latest sound information on the estrogen-depression connection. Given the large numbers of women affected by these issues and the rapid growth in research, I expect that many of those women will derive considerable benefit by keeping the book handy as an essential and ongoing reference and guide.

—Gary Small, MD
Los Angeles, California
June 1, 2006

Introduction

Throughout history, the moods of women have been recognized as distinct from those of men. In ancient Egypt, there was a record of a condition called *hysteria* as early as 1900 BC. This disorder of mood was attributed to the "wandering of the uterus." With time, the definition of hysteria evolved. In the Middle Ages, hysteria was associated with witchcraft, demonic possession, and fanatical religious beliefs. Later it came to be associated with the female sex and described a mental and nervous disorder arising from intense anxiety. Although it could affect men, it was most commonly diagnosed in young women, typically between the ages of fourteen and twenty-five. These women demonstrated lack of control over their emotions and behavior. Furthermore, it was believed that hysteria was less frequent after the age of twenty-five and uncommon after the age of forty-five.

As we review these historical descriptions of women and mood, we are struck by the keen observation of one thing—the developmental time line when the moods of women change. At around the age of fourteen, if not a little earlier, girls become women. They experience puberty and enter a period in which they can reproduce. This new phase is accompanied by a surge of hormones. Then another change begins in the late twenties or early thirties, when women's chances of getting pregnant begin to decline due to a subtle drop in their estrogen and progesterone levels. Finally, perimenopause begins somewhere in the forties for the typical woman, ushering in a dramatic decline in estrogen that will eventually result in menopause. Despite their antiquated explanations, observers of hysteria got the general time line correct regarding women's changes in mood. These changes parallel the hormonal fluctuations across a lifetime that can result in a roller coaster of emotions and physical changes.

Gender Differences

Do women more frequently ride a roller coaster of mood, taking more dips and turns than men? How about in your own life, or in the lives of your female family members, friends, or coworkers? Do you find that more women struggle with depression than men? Most likely the answer to these questions is yes. And this is not only true for American women. Worldwide studies indicate that women are twice as likely as men to experience depression. In the United States alone, the lifetime prevalence of a major depressive disorder is 21 percent for women and 13 percent for men (Halbreich and Kahn 2001). Depression is the leading cause of disability for women in the world. This is particularly true for women between the ages of eighteen and forty-five, and it is true for women in both developed and developing countries (Halbreich and Kahn 2001; Steiner, Dunn, and Born 2003). In this book, we will examine depression in women and discover why it is different for women than men. In particular, we will examine how hormones uniquely influence the risk of depression in women across their life spans.

Questions, Answers & Our Intention

Just how much does estrogen really affect a person's mood? One surprising statistic is that of the depressed women at inpatient psychiatric hospitals, 41 percent are admitted on the day before or the first day of menses (Arpels 1996). There are other questions we might ask: Are teenage girls moodier than boys? Does premenstrual syndrome (PMS) really exist? Are women moody as a result of PMS? Can PMS look like clinical depression, a condition best known as *major depression*? Why do some women suffer from postpartum depression, while others do not? What is perimenopause, and when does it occur? Why are women more at risk than men for depression and possibly for dementia in later life? Should postmenopausal women receive hormone replacement therapy? Are there medical risks, like cancer, associated with hormone replacement therapy?

In this book, we will address these types of questions and other concerns while exploring the connection between estrogen and mood across a woman's life span. As neuropsychologists, we see a variety of clients for both psychotherapy and memory assessment. We have met all types of women who suffer from emotional distress and have wondered how it might be linked to hormones. We became interested in better understanding the estrogen-depression connection because our female clients often complained of mood or cognitive issues, such as depression, anxiety, and poor memory and concentration. Yet there was no apparent disease process, like dementia or major depression, in these clients. Our curiosity about this connection led us to develop a research protocol to investigate how estrogen might impact women's emotional and cognitive functioning. We have published and presented some of our results from this research. We now want to share an overview of this field and our research with everyone—clients and professionals alike—in *The Estrogen-Depression Connection*.

In the upcoming chapters, we are going to explore why estrogen has a tremendous effect on mood. We will begin by describing the role of estrogen in the female brain and will then discuss how estrogen levels rise steadily from the onset of puberty, reach a peak during the twenties, and significantly fluctuate throughout the life span. We will discuss how these fluctuating levels put women at risk for developing depression, premenstrual syndrome (PMS), and premenstrual dysphoric disorder (PMDD). In addition, we will focus on how the imbalance of estrogen levels can result in severe mood changes during pregnancy and postpartum periods. Finally, we will explore how mood and cognition can be affected by declining estrogen levels during the perimenopause-to-postmenopause transition. We hope that the ideas we present here will help spark a much-needed discussion about the estrogen-depression connection. But most of all, we hope that we are providing useful information to anyone who may be suffering.

CHAPTER 1

Estrogen & the Female Brain

"I get PMS every month, so I know estrogen can affect my mood, but I had no idea that it might be related to my ongoing symptoms of depression." This is what we often hear from women in our therapy practice when we suggest the connection between estrogen and depression. Lisa was one of these women. When we first met her, she was thirty-nine years old and had been married for three years. With some sadness, she told us that she was reluctant to get married because she sees herself as moody and feels misunderstood, particularly when she is about to start her menstrual cycle. During these times, she often feels depressed and fatigued, has no desire to socialize, and feels out of control. She needs room to breathe and requires a flexible schedule at work in order to function at her best capacity during these periods.

After trying several things to treat her depression, she found some relief taking a combination of two antidepressants. When she initially thought about individual psychotherapy, she doubted a therapist would really understand how these symptoms fluctuate each month. Then Lisa heard us speak at a local seminar. She approached us and asked about a referral for therapy. She also asked about the possible connection between estrogen and depression in her own life.

As she began therapy, Lisa was primarily concerned with symptoms of depression, including sadness, fatigue, and insomnia, which would last for two or three hours each night. Her husband thought her symptoms were due to work-related stress, but this seemed too simplistic an explanation. Stress can contribute to depression, but it would not account for her fluctuating depressive symptoms each month. Antidepressants were not effective in easing her symptoms, so after some thought, we didn't feel it was appropriate to simply encourage her to continue the antidepressants without addressing the underlying emotional issues and the possible hormonal causes of her depression. We ended up recommending ongoing individual psychotherapy and combining her antidepressants with hormonal replacement.

Had we met Lisa forty or fifty years ago, we would have approached it differently. During that period, it was widely thought that estrogen only served a reproductive role. We now know more. There has been an explosion of research suggesting that the brain is greatly affected by estrogen. These effects are widespread, affecting learning and memory, sensitivity to pain, and emotional homeostasis. When we say *homeostasis*, we are talking about a state of balance, in this case, emotional. This is difficult to achieve given women's fluctuating hormone levels, particularly from puberty to menopause. When these hormone levels do not reach a balance, women are more at risk for developing depression. As scientists and researchers gradually came to understand the relationship between estrogen and depression, they began wondering if some depression in women was due to the role of estrogen in the female brain.

NOTE: *We ask you as readers to please keep in mind that while the stories we will present in this book are based on actual women, they are composites of many women rather than a specific client or friend. All names are fictional.*

What Is Estrogen?

Lisa thought she had a relatively good understanding of estrogen. Like many women, she gathered isolated slices of information about it from her mom, female friends, personal experience, and classes taken in high school or college.

But as we worked with her, she was surprised to learn the ways that estrogen also influences the brains and moods of women.

As we share some of the same thoughts we explored with Lisa, it will be helpful for you to have an understanding of what estrogen is and how it impacts the brain. Put simply, estrogen is a female sex hormone that is primarily produced by the ovaries, although smaller amounts are also produced by a structure in the brain called the *adrenal cortex*. There are three naturally occurring forms of estrogen: estradiol, estriol, and estrone. We will discuss these specific forms of estrogen later in the book, but for the present time we will refer to them collectively as *estrogen*. While estrogens are present in both men and women, women have them in significantly higher quantities than men. These estrogens promote the development of female secondary sexual characteristics, such as breast development. They are also involved in controlling the menstrual cycle, which is why most oral forms of birth control contain estrogens. But the effect of estrogen begins even before birth.

Estrogen & Early Brain Organization

You know the old expression, "Before you were a twinkle in my eye"? Well, estrogen makes its first impact on brain development before a mother even realizes that she's going to give birth to a baby. These earliest effects are called *organizational operations* because they organize the architecture of the brain in a way that creates sex differences in our brains and behavior (Halbreich and Kahn 2001; Schechter 1999).

Imagine, for example, that a civil engineer is hired to build two subway systems, one for men and one for women. He needs different blueprints to build each of these systems to fit the different needs of men and women. In a similar way, the brain of the prenatal infant works as an engineer who needs blueprints to modify subway tracks to fit a male or female body. These blueprints come from the unborn infant's hormones and represent the organizational operations that modify the brain's structure and neural circuitry. This blueprint, so to speak, differentiates the female from the male body, brain, and neurodevelopment, particularly in ways that influence mood and behavior, such as by determining the way in which the molecules that receive estrogen are positioned in the brain, which can contribute to estrogen's impact on mood.

Estrogen Receptors

Imagine the subway system again. Both the female and male tracks have frequent stops where passengers are able to use the phone—that is, they can communicate a message. Many of these messages will likely involve statements about how they are feeling. Some "messages" may indicate to friends or family that they are feeling happy, others sad, and others nervous or simply ambivalent.

There are molecules in our brain called *estrogen receptors* that act in a similar way. They are organized like these subway stops, but they are densely packed into various regions of the brain that greatly influence mood and behavior. One of the areas with a high density of these estrogen receptors in women is the *limbic system.* The limbic system is the switchboard of our internal subway and is responsible for emotional processing (Lee and McEwen 2001; Soares, Poitras, and Prouty 2003). The functions of several brain structures in this complicated switchboard are summarized in table 1.1 (O'Connell 2005; Wieck 1996):

TABLE 1.1: **LIMBIC SYSTEM**

Limbic Structures	Activity and Function
Hypothalamus	Coordinates sleep and energy
Prefrontal lobes	Directs attention and behavior
Amygdala	Mediates mood and levels of motivation
Hippocampus and nucleus accumbens	Provides resilience to chronic stress and regulates emotional behaviors

Because these structures have a high density of estrogen receptors, they are going to be easily impacted by changes in estrogen. The estrogen-dense structures listed in this table govern sleep, motivation, resilience, and mood, areas in which depressive symptoms can be expressed. Because, unlike men, women are likely to experience fluctuations in estrogen throughout their life span, they may be more biologically predisposed toward a greater risk of depression. This predisposition is based not only on the activity of estrogen prior to birth, but also on some effects that occur after birth.

Estrogen & the Brain After Birth

Estrogen exerts a second and different type of effect on the female brain after birth and throughout a woman's life on what are called *activational operations.* There is no clearly defined point when organizational operations end and activational operations begin. This is mostly because estrogen continues to influence the organization of a woman's brain throughout the early years of her development. For the sake of simplicity, we can say that activational operations usually begin with puberty and proceed into adulthood. In general, these operations are more temporary and reversible, allowing some control of changes in brain structure and biochemistry that are involved in mood, cognition, and behavior.

The way these activational operations occur is somewhat complicated but similar to the process of going to an ATM. Whenever we need money, many of us visit the ATM at our local bank. We enter the bank, insert our ATM card into the machine, and punch in our PIN. We then request a certain amount of money, which changes the balance of our checking or savings account.

This is similar to what happens with estrogen's activational operations. Estrogen circulates through the body and then passes through cell membranes, much as we decide to enter the bank. We insert our ATM card into the machine; estrogen passes through the cell membranes and binds to the estrogen receptors that are specifically designed to receive it. As we have to enter our specific PIN to locate the right account, so estrogen also has particular types of receptors that it needs to activate. (The two that have been identified to date are called ERα and ERβ [Sherwin 2003].) Once we enter the amount we want to withdraw, our bank account content is changed. In a similar fashion, the binding of estrogen to the receptor creates a structural change in the receptor so that it can regulate how certain genes are expressed, that is, how they communicate and operate. This includes the genes responsible for mood and behavior (Wieck 1996; Woolley 1999). This process is repeated as the levels of estrogen rise and fall throughout a woman's reproductive life cycle, changing the structure and biochemistry of the brain.

The long-term effect of estrogen is akin to what happens with volcanoes. You can see the way a volcanic landscape has changed with the rise and fall of magma. When it is hot, magma forms and reshapes the land, later to cool and solidify. But this configuration is only temporary; when more magma emerges, it will redesign and alter the land.

In a similar way, the continued rise and fall of estrogen consistently forms, reshapes, and changes the landscape of the connections and biochemistry of the brain. This suggests that the brain is relatively plastic and changeable. Just as magma can reshape surrounding land, so too estrogen can exert activational operations that remodel the connections between neurons, change the structure and density of the neurons themselves, and contribute to the creation of new neurons that are directly involved in a woman's mood (McEwen 2001; Payne 2003).

Estrogen as a Protector & Communicator

The activational operations of estrogen include not only changing the neurons responsible for mood, but also regulating inflammation and protecting brain cells from dying. Throughout our brains, there are particles called *free radicals* that act like termites, destroying our brain cells. They come from a variety of sources. Genetics might dictate whether we have more or less of them. Poor nutrition might increase their presence. Recent illnesses or life stressors might bring on an army of them. Regardless of where they come from, these free radicals bring increased inflammation, resulting in the death of some brain cells. One of the roles of estrogen, however, is to protect the brain from some of this cell death by clearing out the free radicals. It can act as the exterminator, so to speak.

As we will see in chapter 7, estrogen can play a role in protecting the brain and preserving cognitive functioning. Estrogen also enhances the blood flow in the brain (Small 1998). This has the effect of "powering up" the brain, or in a sense improving efficiency. With greater blood flow comes an increase in the level of communication between brain cells. This can result in more productive thinking: if we are more attentive, we can take in new information, and we are more likely to learn this new information and recall it later. You could say that our attention span and memory are better tuned. Clearly, estrogen has the ability to remodel or restructure the brain. It also has the ability to alter the way our brain cells communicate.

Estrogen & Neurotransmitters

Remember the stops along our subway system, where we can hop off to make a phone call, that is, to send a message? Imagine that estrogen has the ability to send a text message via cell phone. Estrogen helps direct the creation of the structures we mentioned earlier, and it also sends those biochemical messages. The biochemical messages, much like the text messages of our cell phone, are sent via chemicals known as *neurotransmitters.* Just as we need to have the right phone number to send the text message, we also need to have the correct neurotransmitter.

A neuron releases neurotransmitters into a gap called the *synaptic cleft* where they are picked up by another neuron. Among other things, this communication between neurons regulates mood and behavior. Our mood can be altered when the level of these neurotransmitters fluctuates outside their normal levels, which may vary for each individual. Mood also depends on how many of the neurotransmitters are created, broken down, or left in the synaptic cleft. Again, it is similar to the cell-phone call. When you are having a bad day and call your best friend, she can cheer you up. But if you call the wrong number, a stranger will most likely hang up on you. The correct phone number, or coded neurotransmitter, can make a substantial difference in your mood.

One of the functions of estrogen is to alter the concentration and availability of several neurotransmitters involved in the regulation of mood. These neurotransmitters include dopamine, norepinephrine, acetylcholine, glutamate, GABA (gamma-aminobutyric acid), and serotonin. By controlling the creation, release, and breakdown of these neurotransmitters, estrogen acts similarly to antidepressants (Halbreich and Kahn 2001; Payne 2003). So estrogen may regulate depression and serve as the brain's natural antidepressant simply due to its influence on neurotransmitters.

SEROTONIN & DEPRESSION

In the context of depression, serotonin is perhaps the most widely studied neurotransmitter. A deficiency of serotonin is the reigning theory about the biological cause of depression. The lack of availability of serotonin may occur at any level, including the following:

· Poor serotonin production and release

· Overactivity of receptors that remove serotonin from the synaptic cleft

· Overactivity of the chemicals that break serotonin down

This is why most antidepressant treatments seek to increase the availability of serotonin using any means possible. Medications like Prozac (fluoxetine) and Zoloft (sertraline HCL) block the *uptake*, that is, the absorption, of serotonin so more is available in the synaptic cleft. Other medications, like Nardil (phenelzine), hamper the breakdown of serotonin. In chapter 6, on treatment, we will talk more about the role of serotonin in the alleviation of depression.

SEROTONIN & ESTROGEN

One reason estrogen may serve as a natural antidepressant is because it naturally affects all levels of serotonin functioning. Many of the neurons in the brain that release serotonin contain estrogen receptors. This means they let estrogen determine the availability, concentration, and use of serotonin. The following is a short list of the ways estrogen influences serotonin:

· **Serotonin creation:** Estrogen displaces *tryptophan*, one of the building blocks of serotonin, from its binding sites, which increases its availability for creating more serotonin (Warnock, Bundren, and Morris 1998; Zweifel and O'Brien 1997).

· **Serotonin breakdown:** To prevent too much breakdown of serotonin, estrogen interferes with enzymes that deconstruct serotonin. One of these enzymes is *monoamine oxidase* (MAO) (Chakravorty and Halbreich 1997; Soares, Poitras, and Prouty 2003).

- **Serotonin uptake**: Estrogen increases the retrieval of serotonin by increasing the density of binding sites and receptors that are friendly to serotonin, particularly in areas that control mood and cognition (Fink et al. 1996; Huttner and Shepherd 2003).

This short list indicates a high correlation between estrogen and serotonin levels (Huttner and Shepherd 2003). If serotonin was a medicinal drug being created in a lab, this list would show how estrogen makes more of the raw elements necessary for creating the drug, removes any materials that may interfere with making this medicine, and provides more containers for gathering the drug.

For example, women who have their ovaries removed (*ovariectomies*) experience a decrease in serotonin activity. This results in reduced serotonin binding, creation, and expression. If these same women use hormone replacement therapy to supplement their estrogen levels, they experience an increase in serotonin activity (Amin, Canli, and Epperson 2005; Joffe and Cohen 1998). In other words, estrogen can act like the key to the medicine cabinet. It can help us access and modify the serotonin we need to elevate our moods.

The effect of estrogen on organizational and activational operations is similar to the effect of the ocean on the landscape. Those who go to the beach for a day often do not see the impact on the beach, rocks, or surrounding land because it is not a simple rise or fall of the waves that carves out the landscape. Rather, those who sit, listen, and watch the tide over a period of days and nights are likely to see that it is the constant fluctuation, the ebb and flow of the waves, that leaves the land different over time. In a similar fashion, it is not simply a high or low level of estrogen that alters mood or behavior, but rather the constant ebb and flow of estrogen throughout the reproductive life cycle. Estrogen's function is to maintain homeostasis, but the repeated ebb and flow of estrogen may create a destabilizing effect that offsets the homeostatic effect of estrogen and prompts changes in mood. It is this rise and fall of estrogen that alters the structural and neurotransmitter landscape in a way that directly influences a woman's vulnerability to depression and other mood disorders. Because these changes are part of the reproductive life cycle, they are not abnormal in and of themselves, but they may represent triggers for the development of depressive symptoms. Part of these changes involve neurotransmitters, but other biochemicals are also involved.

Other Biochemical Effects of Estrogen

The effect of estrogen on mood is not only mediated by neurotransmitters, but also by other *biochemicals*, including those responsible for the growth or repair of neurons and those related to an elevation of mood.

Biochemicals for Growth & Repair

Estrogen stimulates the expression and release of chemicals called *nerve growth factors*. One of these chemicals is the *brain-derived neurotrophic factor* (BDNF). This biochemical influences the growth, connection, and repair of neurons involved in serotonin and other cells concerned with depression (Payne 2003; Joffe and Cohen 1998). Estrogen seems to regulate the expression of BDNF; as estrogen levels drop in response to hormonal changes in the reproductive cycle, there is a critical decrease in BDNF. This decrease in BDNF has also been noted in women who suffer from depression, suggesting that BDNF may represent one pathway by which estrogen is related to depression.

Biochemicals for Elevated Moods

Estrogen has a similar role with the expression of a biochemical called *protein kinase C* (PKC). This biochemical has been implicated in mood disorders where people experience either an extreme elevation of their mood (*mania*) or an extreme fluctuation between elevation and depression of mood (*bipolar disorder*). It appears that estrogen increases the expression of PKC and provides an excitatory or antidepressant role in the female body (Payne 2003). For example, the administration of estrogen has been found to create mania in women with a history of bipolar disorder. In other words, those women already susceptible to extreme mood changes may experience an extreme elevation of their mood when taking additional estrogen. This suggests that one of estrogen's natural roles may be to elevate mood and affect. To the extent that estrogen varies or fluctuates, similar to the fluctuations seen in the reproductive life cycle, women may be at greater risk for changes in mood.

Circadian Rhythms

The impact of estrogen on the circadian system represents another area that has only recently received attention for its potential role in depression. Many women with depression have difficulty falling asleep or they wake during the night or earlier than desired. It is largely thought that these sleep difficulties are due to a loss of regulation in the normal circadian rhythms that control sleep timing and quality.

The possibility of a direct effect of estrogen on the human circadian system was first raised by the discovery of a high number of estrogen receptors in a brain structure called the *hypothalamic suprachiasmatic nuclei* (SCN) (Dzaja et al. 2005). This structure contains the pacemaker that generates circadian rhythms, suggesting that the very control center for women's sleep cycles appears to be highly sensitive to the influence of estrogen. We also know that *estrogen replacement therapy* (ERT), in which women are given supplemental estrogen, is an effective treatment for sleep disruption. ERT improves sleep quality, facilitates falling asleep, increases REM sleep, and decreases nighttime restlessness and awakenings (Dzaja et al. 2005; Shin and Shapiro 2003). Women taking ERT have improved sleep and report better mood. We know our moods improve when we get enough sleep. In this case, ERT may have helped these women have better sleep and thereby improved their moods. This suggests an interaction between circadian rhythms and the rhythms of estrogen's rise and fall. Considering the strong relationship between sleep difficulties and depressive symptoms, the control of circadian rhythms may represent another area where estrogen indirectly affects the mood and well-being of women. However, it is less certain that estrogen affects the mood of men.

Estrogen & Men

After hearing about all the ways that estrogen influences mood, many women wonder what effect, if any, estrogen has on men. Estrogen does influence the male brain. The male brain has fewer receptors for estrogen, but it is produced in careful balance with their primary sex hormone, testosterone. This does not mean that men are less sensitive to the effects of estrogen. Quite the contrary; as men get older, their testosterone is increasingly converted to estrogen. This disrupts the delicate hormonal balance and either directly or indirectly accounts for many of the diseases and physical changes that middle-aged men begin experiencing, including depression, fatigue, abdominal weight gain, decreased libido, erectile dysfunction, prostate disease, and heart disease. The hormonal imbalance and elevation of estrogen levels leads to further aging and potential emotional breakdowns. Thus the changes and disruptions in estrogen's equilibrium incur a wide range of health problems for men as well as women.

Conclusion

Estrogen has multiple effects on the female brain, ranging from its impact on organizational operations that occur prenatally to structural and biochemical operations that occur during maturation and adulthood. Many of these effects have been implicated in depression, leading many experts to conclude that estrogen functions as one of the brain's natural antidepressants. In fact, it performs roles that are similar to current treatments for depression such as antidepressant medications and sleep therapy.

The antidepressant effect of estrogen is not due to any one system or mode of operation. Rather, its effect on mood is likely due to the interaction between systems. For example, our client Lisa, whom you met earlier in the chapter, may be predisposed to experiencing depression based on family history or genetics, but she may also be experiencing depression during this phase of life because of an imbalance in her estrogen levels. As we delve into additional clinical composites of real cases in this book, it will become apparent that part of estrogen's influence on any given woman is reflective of where she is developmentally in the reproductive life cycle. We will show evidence suggesting that the serotonin system is involved in premenstrual mood symptoms, while postpartum depression may be related to estrogen's effects on BDNF (Payne 2003). This makes it difficult to say that estrogen influences mood through one particular pathway or mechanism, and the danger is that women may therefore dismiss the role of estrogen altogether.

Estrogen should no longer be seen as simply a part of the reproductive cycle. In the introduction, we told you that almost half of the depressed women in psychiatric hospitals are admitted the day before or of their menses. This suggests that many women are sensitive to the destabilizing effects of estrogen's fluctuations at normal stages of their reproductive cycle. This may account for the changes in mood and elevations in depression that women often experience throughout the reproductive life cycle as estrogen levels rise and fall. To really understand the impact of estrogen on mood, it is crucial to examine those times when estrogen levels fluctuate or change in a woman's life, particularly during puberty, premenstrual stages, postpartum, and peri- and postmenopausal states. In the following chapters, we'll discuss these periods of hormonal fluctuation or estrogen instability that may leave some women more vulnerable to depression.

CHAPTER 2

Puberty

The tears felt cold on her cheeks. She was trying to hold them back, but they seemed to fall of their own accord. She wiped beneath her eyes and noticed streaks of mascara on her hands. "Great, Madison, you must look like a mess," she whispered to herself.

The truth was that Madison was not completely certain why she was crying. Over the past couple of months, she had been struggling with insomnia, and her energy had become so depleted that she wanted to sleep every minute. Just last week she had received a detention because she had overslept and arrived late to school. She was also losing interest in some of the activities that she had previously enjoyed, like her drama program after school. She particularly enjoyed the wry and subtle humor in the Shakespearean play they were working on. But now she simply wanted to come home after her final class. She had even lost her appetite for her favorite foods, which was slightly alarming because her friends once teased her about her ravenous appetite. Her mother and teachers had become concerned, but Madison was not really certain how to respond when they asked what was bothering her.

Now she was outside, standing in the snow. She looked up at the sky, at the sharpness of the stars, at the moon as it cast its evening light, making the snow crystals sparkle across the yard. Every breath was visible in the night air. She almost dared not speak out of fear that the cold would break her words.

She had just told her family and friends that she needed to step outside. It was her fourteenth birthday, and everyone had gathered to celebrate with her. According to her teachers and the parents of her friends, she was entering the prime years of her life. It was supposed to be a time filled with first kisses and gossiping with friends, a time when her greatest concern should be whether or not she was wearing outfits that were in style. And yet, here she was, caught between the sadness and isolation she felt inside and the warmth and joy that she was supposed to express on the outside.

She turned around slowly and saw her solitary trail of footprints in the snow. They led back to her home, only a few hundred feet behind her, where she could hear the mirth and laughter of her friends. The glow from the windows was a beacon of warmth, inviting her back. But it seemed like such a contradiction to enter such warmth and yet inwardly feel so cold and alone.

She whispered, "Why am I so sad all the time?"

The Sad Truth

Madison's experience is not uncommon among adolescent girls. Quite the contrary; many teenage girls begin experiencing an increase in sadness, loneliness, and other symptoms of depression around Madison's age. And they find themselves asking similar questions about why their mood has changed so much. A girl who was once happy during her childhood can become sad, sleepless, and anxious during her adolescence.

It is not a coincidence that this change frequently occurs when most women enter puberty. The social, psychological, and hormonal changes that accompany puberty increase women's risk for depression and other mood disorders. In the past, many parents and physicians attributed these changes to the instability of simply being an adolescent. If you are the parent of a teenager, you know firsthand how adolescents can be fickle, temperamental, and rebellious. These characteristics appear to be fertile ground for depression. Many mothers may have talked with their neighbors or friends about their own period of adolescent angst, leading them to conclude that this is a normal phase of female development.

The danger is that this fails to place adolescent depression, particularly for a woman, in the context of her biology and developmental changes. To avoid this danger, it is important for all women, to understand not only how estrogen influences the emergence of depression during adolescence, but also what depression looks like during this phase of life. This may change how some girls perceive their entry into puberty, how some parents raise their teenage girls, and how some women look back at their adolescence. This understanding begins by realizing that the period of puberty and adolescence may be the first time that estrogen specifically influences the mood of women.

Puberty & the Emergence of Depression

Puberty appears to be the earliest point when clear differences in depression emerge between men and women. As we mentioned in the first chapter, women are at significantly greater risk for depression than men. The likelihood of having a major depressive disorder—or other depressive conditions like *dysthymia* (chronic depression) and *seasonal affective disorder* (depression that only occurs in the fall and winter months)—is almost two times higher for women than men at any point in a lifetime (Parker and Brotchie 2004).

This may not be altogether startling when you look at your own relationships. Most likely, you are able to name more women than men who have gone through periods of depression. But if you compare boys and girls rather than adult men and women, the picture of depression looks drastically different. When we present at seminars and conferences, many individuals find it surprising that differences in depression do not appear until puberty. They are amazed, as were we, that boys and girls during childhood either have similar rates of depression or that boys have slightly elevated levels of depression (Angold, Costello, and Worthman 1998; Steiner, Dunn, and Born 2003). In other words, if you have a young daughter, then prior to puberty she is likely to have either the same level of depression as her male friends or slightly lower levels.

It is not completely certain why boys might be at a slightly higher risk for depression when they are younger. Testosterone may have something to do with it. Testosterone may serve as a chemical buffer, or shock absorber, against depression. But young boys may not be able to fully benefit from this buffering role until puberty, when testosterone levels rise. The relative lack of testosterone in young boys may therefore elevate their chances of becoming depressed.

What is clear, however, is that something changes for girls between the ages of twelve and fourteen. Beginning at this age, the proportion of depression shifts so that women are twice as likely to experience depression as men. It is at this point that over 20 percent of adolescent women and only 10 percent of adolescent men experience major depression. This suggests a clear point of transition in the development of girls—a transition that makes them susceptible to an increased risk for depression.

Why the Rise in Depression in Women?

Multiple factors likely contribute to the appearance and timing of this rise in depression in adolescent girls. Part of it may simply be how teenage women and men have been socialized to express their emotions in different ways. We'll use the communication styles of two teenagers to illustrate some differences in style of expression.

Styles of Expression

Mark and Renee are thirteen-year-old fraternal twins living in the same household. Their parents consistently remark to each other how ironic it is that these two teenagers can be so similar in appearance and genetic makeup but so different in their style of communication. When talking with Mark or overhearing his conversations with friends, they have noticed that the content of his language is more task-oriented, assertive, and focused on specific behaviors or activities. But when they talk with Renee, they notice that her conversations are more passive, people-oriented, and emotional in content.

As teenagers, Mark and Renee's different communication styles may reflect how they have been taught by society, parents, and peers to express themselves differently. When researchers have analyzed the conversations between parents and children in the home, they've found that parents talk more about the emotional aspect of events with their daughters than with their sons (Kuebli and Fivush 1992). This suggests that girls are generally more socialized to talk about and express their feelings. Like many boys, Mark's focus on specific behaviors and tasks, with a disproportionate focus on the physical relative to the emotional, can distract him from difficult moods and provide a sense of agency and control over his environment that enhances his self-esteem and buffers against depression. Renee's style of expression, on the other hand, places greater emphasis on being emotionally responsive and sensitive to others, which may leave her with a limited sense of having power or control over her environment. Because she is socialized into greater passivity and may have to suppress her confidence or independence, she may be more susceptible to lower self-esteem and depression.

Granted, Mark and Renee's styles of expression will not generalize to every teenage boy and girl. And neither process is better or worse than the other. Mark's approach may make him less prone to depression because it fosters a sense of power and independence that distances him from sadness. But it may also lead him to express emotions behaviorally, such as by acting out when he feels an unpleasant emotion. Renee's focus on emotional responsiveness and gentleness may lead to social fluidity and success. But it may also make her more passive and leave her feeling bereft of personal power, which are key aspects of depression.

Cultural Differences

At this point, you may be asking, "Okay, that's well and good, but doesn't society and culture play a large role here? Are adolescent girls more depressed than boys because of traditional roles girls are expected to assume?"

There is a lot of truth in this statement, although it should first be noted that cultural values about gender roles are changing. There are hints that jobs, sports, and family roles are slowly becoming less likely to create distinctions between men and women. However, traditional thinking still exists about the roles permitted to boys and girls. Even though cultures vary in their sex-role traditions, there are some universal stereotypes about men and women. In a large-scale study, Williams and Best (1982) asked 2,800 college students from thirty countries to check off adjectives they believed best described men and women. Men were consistently said to be adventurous, strong, dominant, assertive, task-oriented, aggressive, and independent. In contrast, women were consistently described as sensitive, gentle, emotional, sentimental, submissive, and people-oriented. Despite our best efforts, these gender roles still appear to be ingrained in our cultures. Women are still more likely than men to take on caregiving responsibilities, and jokes are still made about some women who take on positions of leadership. It is hard for adolescent girls to be immune to these roles, expectations, and jokes, even if parents and teachers try to broaden their expectations. When young girls enter into puberty and experience their first period, it may feel like the time when they are expected to adopt some of these traditional gender roles. At times, these roles may create a conflict with their personal desires, ambitions, and dreams. This conflict easily becomes the seed for depression.

Something Is Missing

But something is still missing in our formula for adolescent depression. So far, we have discussed the importance of cultural values and how adolescent girls may approach their emotions differently than boys. Yet neither completely explains adolescent depression. There is still a large element that needs to be addressed because it is central to the appearance of depression in girls during adolescence.

To determine what this missing factor might be, Adrian Angold and his colleagues from Emory University and Duke University Medical Center conducted two studies on 4,500 children between the ages of nine and sixteen who were from the public school systems of eleven counties in North Carolina. In their first study (Angold, Costello, and Worthman 1998), they found that boys had higher rates of depressive disorders prior to midpuberty, but girls developed higher rates than boys after midpuberty, beginning at around age thirteen. In their second study (Angold et al. 1999), they attempted to isolate the major determinant for the increased rate of depression in girls. According to their results, it was not the age at which children reached puberty nor was it the psychosocial changes occurring around them that accounted for most of the depression in girls. Instead, the primary contributor was the change in their estrogen levels. In a sense, the "active ingredient" in the rise of depression in adolescent women was the elevation or change in estrogen concentrations that are experienced during *menarche*, the beginning of menstruation.

Changes in Estrogen Levels

This finding makes sense considering how estrogen levels change during adolescence. Prior to puberty, concentrations of estrogen are relatively low, but with the onset of puberty, the female brain is exposed to monthly surges of estrogen. This sudden elevation in estrogen seems to usher in a sequence of changes, including the following:

- A growth spurt in height and weight between seven and eleven years of age, with continued physical growth for several years
- The budding of breasts at around age ten
- The maturation of pubic hair and sexual organs
- The beginning of menstruation
- The broadening of the hips
- The growth of fatty deposits

These changes typically occur over a period of four to five years. The onset of these changes now occurs at an earlier age than in previous generations. In fact, Dr. Steiner and colleagues (2003) report that the age of menarche has declined four months per decade since 1850. This is largely thought to be due to environmental factors, like the improvements in health, nutrition, and other sociocultural factors brought about by urbanization.

Regardless of when menarche occurs, the onset of puberty marks the beginning of sex-based differences in the rate of depression. In particular, it is the new fluctuation in estrogen levels that may precipitate the first onset of depressive symptoms (Halbreich and Kahn 2001). Prior to the onset of menarche, estrogen remains at a balanced and uninterrupted state. With the onset, this balance is disrupted, creating an unstable hormonal environment that makes girls more susceptible to depression. For some teenage girls, the simple fluctuation in estrogen levels at this age is sufficient in itself to lead to depression. For other girls who might be predisposed to depression through their family history or certain environmental factors, like sex-based roles, the rapid changes in estrogen levels tip them over a certain threshold. The main thing to remember is that it is during this pubertal stage that a girl's body and brain are experiencing the rapid cycling of estrogen. And it is this rapid cycling of estrogen that creates a destabilizing effect that leaves a girl more vulnerable to the risk of depression.

This is significant because it argues that depression is intimately tied to biological changes in the levels of hormones. It is specifically the high level of fluctuation in estrogen that increases a girl's risk for depression. All adolescent girls experience these fluctuations, and it is true that some girls do not experience depression. But some girls may be more predisposed to react to this rise and fall of estrogen with mood disturbances. Therefore, at the time when teenage boys are profiting from the buffering role of testosterone against depression, the hormonal environment of adolescent girls places them at greater risk for depression.

KINDLING

Perhaps the example of kindling will be helpful. Let's say that you wanted to escape from the city for a weekend of camping. You head up to the mountains, set up your tent, and then collect some firewood. As night approaches, you decide it might be nice to start a campfire. No one expects you to start a fire by simply dropping large pieces of wood on the fire pit and throwing a match on it. Instead, most campers light small pieces of wood called kindling that can burn long enough to ignite larger pieces of wood.

This use of kindling is similar to what happens with estrogen during puberty. On their own, the body and brain of an adolescent female are unlikely to develop depression. They would prefer the balance, or homeostasis, which we described in chapter 1. But when something like estrogen cycling disrupts this balance, the fire of depression may be ignited. In a sense, the cyclic fluctuation of estrogen acts like kindling to ignite larger changes in mood. These estrogen changes do not ignite depression in all women, but they may trigger a sequence of events that make it easier for depression to occur, particularly among girls who are more vulnerable.

SEROTONIN

One of the ways these changes in estrogen influence depression is through the neurotransmitter systems discussed in chapter 1. The newly fluctuating levels of estrogen introduce a significant change into the hormonal environment. This in turn encourages a change in the brain's neurotransmitters and other biological systems.

The neurotransmitter system that is particularly affected is the serotonin system (Steiner, Dunn, and Born 2003). This system appears to mature at a faster rate than some of the other neurotransmitter systems, so that even early on in a girl's development, this system is more responsive and sensitive to the messages given by estrogen. You may recall from chapter 1 how these messages alter the creation, availability, and activity of serotonin in a way that can elevate or reduce depression (Steiner, Dunn, and Born 2003). In its normal and stable state, estrogen acts to make a high level of serotonin available. But during puberty, the rise and fall of estrogen may leave an insufficient level of serotonin in the brain, making it more susceptible to depression.

This is similar to the way sleep works in our bodies. Sleep is a precious commodity. When you get a sufficient amount of sleep, it helps protect your body from illness. When you get less sleep, you immediately become more vulnerable to infection, illness, stress, and depression. In the same way, normal levels of estrogen help protect the brain from depression by regulating the activity of serotonin. When estrogen is disrupted from its normal levels and thrown into a state of flux, much like what happens in puberty, it leaves the brain at greater risk for depression.

HPA AXIS

In addition to the serotonin system, there is a hormonal system that is maturing in adolescents that is also sensitive to changes in estrogen levels. This hormonal system is called the *hypothalamic pituitary adrenal axis* (HPA axis), which refers to a set of interactions among glands, hormones, and parts of the brain that control our reactions to stress. In a sense, the HPA axis can be thought of as the body's energy regulator because it is ultimately responsible for controlling most of the hormones, nervous-system activity, and energy use in the human body. If the HPA axis is disrupted, it can lead to symptoms of depression.

At this point, you may be wondering where estrogen fits in. This HPA system is highly responsive to estrogen, so changes in estrogen levels may disrupt this system and render girls more vulnerable to depression (Young and Altemus 2004). How does this work? For adolescent girls in the middle of puberty, this system is still maturing, making adolescent women unable to adaptively respond to stress and therefore more susceptible to sadness and other depressive symptoms. Although the normal job of the HPA axis is to control the brain's reactions to stress, this role is disrupted when estrogen levels change or fluctuate, making adolescent women more vulnerable to stressors.

This is similar to what happens when we try to regulate stress in our everyday lives. Normally, most of us have built-in methods for managing stress. But any change in overall functioning can upset this balance. A demanding e-mail can disrupt our work schedule, a sick child can cause a loss of sleep, and a natural disaster can replace our optimism with hopelessness. These unexpected stressors can lower our threshold for handling stress in general. In a similar way, changes in the normal levels of estrogen, such as those that occur at the onset of puberty, can change the sensitivity of the HPA system, disrupting its ability to regulate stress and stabilize mood.

THE MAIN POINT

If this discussion of serotonin and the HPA axis left you glassy eyed and wondering what's on television, let's return to the main point. Depression occurs during adolescence in large part because of the changes in estrogen levels that occur during midpuberty. During the first five years of menstruation, a girl's body is almost violently thrown into hormonal shock. Her body and brain are exposed to monthly surges of estrogen that disrupt her normal internal balance. The more these estrogen levels fluctuate, the greater her risk for depression.

EARLY & LATE BLOOMERS

This may explain why the rates of depression are higher among girls who develop puberty earlier than their peers. Many of the girls who can be considered "early bloomers" have higher levels of estrogen and experience the flux of estrogen earlier than their peers. This may account for their tendency to experience more depression earlier than those who "bloom" later. Psychological and social factors may also influence depression in these girls. A girl who enters puberty earlier than her peers must face the reactions of others to her development. Society's expectations for her may change with the onset of puberty, and she may lose the support from her peers who are not experiencing similar changes (Kaltiala-Heino, Kosunen, and Rimpela 2003; Kaltiala-Heino et al. 2003). She may have to look to older women for support and may therefore feel isolated from her peer group. Frequently, adolescent women who experience puberty early struggle with low self-esteem and negative self-image because it is difficult to adjust to a new body image. They also feel alone in the process.

Ironically, the reverse happens for boys. Early maturation appears to protect boys from depression. For adolescent boys, the development of a growth spurt and the maturation of secondary sexual features, such as the deepening of the voice and the development of facial hair, are all associated with greater maturity. These developments are perceived with respect by peers and welcomed by society, which creates a network of support that is different from the isolation experienced by early-blooming women.

As this implies, it is the late-blooming boys who are more likely to experience depression. There is considerable stigma associated with late development among boys. Social isolation occurs from being at a different maturational level than other boys and most girls, who generally reach puberty earlier than boys. Many of these boys experience the masculine drive for competition but experience a sense of defeat and humiliation because they feel left behind, as if something is biologically flawed about them. This also decreases their sense of self-confidence and jeopardizes their ability to feel comfortable in relationships. It seems that self-confidence in both adolescent men and women is influenced by hormonal change.

The Face of Adolescent Depression

At this point, it seems clear that estrogen contributes to the emergence of depression among girls in puberty. But, what does depression actually look like in adolescence? The effects of estrogen on the mood of women can vary according to a woman's phase of life, with the symptoms of depression looking different in adolescence than in menopause. Granted, some of the core features of depression are shared, and when you utter the word "depression," most everyone assumes a certain working definition with a constellation of symptoms. Many of the following symptoms may come to mind:

- Depressed mood
- Anxiety
- Loss of pleasure in almost all activities
- Irritability
- Significant weight gain or loss
- Feeling slow or inattentive
- Getting too much or too little sleep

- Fatigue or loss of energy
- Feelings of worthlessness
- Feelings of guilt
- Difficulties with concentration
- Thoughts of death
- Self-criticism
- Feeling gloomy

These symptoms characterize what most doctors and psychologists understand to be depression. These are the symptoms that depressed individuals report. However, the profile of depressive symptoms may look different for adolescents than it does for adults. Moreover, the face of adolescent depression appears different in girls than in boys.

Symptoms of Adolescent Depression

The symptoms of depression are generally milder in adolescents than adults, although 15 to 20 percent of teenagers can have serious episodes of depression (Halbreich and Kahn 2001; Hauenstein 2003). Again, true depression is often difficult to diagnose in teenagers because normal adolescent behavior is marked by frequent and rapid fluctuations in mood. However, the more common symptoms of adolescent depression include feeling gloomy and self-critical, withdrawing from pleasurable activities, and experiencing observable changes in appetite, loss of energy, and disrupted sleep.

Remember earlier when we said that not every adolescent girl will develop symptoms of depression, but that the pubertal changes in estrogen increase a girl's risk for depression? We said that estrogen fluctuations alone can be sufficient to contribute to depression in some girls. In others, we mentioned that these fluctuations create a vulnerability that predisposes them to depression, which can be activated when combined with other factors. Some of the particular factors that can interact with estrogen and push teenage girls over the threshold for depression include feelings of defeat, humiliation, and entrapment.

DEFEAT

For many teenagers, defeat represents a challenge to a newly forming sense of power and agency. Some teenagers protect themselves from feelings of defeat and ensure their sense of power by withdrawing from conflict. Others may embrace every opportunity for ambition or competition to assure themselves of their place in the world. In either case, feelings of defeat leave teenagers feeling powerless and inferior.

HUMILIATION

Adolescents are also particularly sensitive to feelings of humiliation. Shame and humiliation are concepts that are central to a sense of identity. For adolescents, this frequently involves a social element, whereby peers, coaches, teachers, or parents appear to hold the teenager up against the yardstick of life and find them wanting. Some teenagers experience humiliation when their peers criticize their clothes or their family's socioeconomic status. Others experience humiliation during pranks that reveal their personal weaknesses.

As a case in point, Molly, who was one of our clients, was deeply sensitive about being adopted and about her symptoms of attention deficit disorder. She was so humiliated by these aspects of herself that she became depressed and vengeful when it seemed like others might use these "weaknesses" against her. She became extremely angry when friends casually mentioned to others that she was adopted or when her boyfriend asked why she was taking medication to help her focus. In a sense, she saw adoption and having an attentional disorder as signs of personal failings, as if she was somehow flawed or defective. Therapy became a tool that helped her to have more grace with herself and to see herself as having positive and negative aspects. But, like Molly, many adolescents have elements of their identity that can make them feel humiliated and ashamed, which can exacerbate their risk for depression, especially when paired with their monthly surges of estrogen.

ENTRAPMENT

Feelings of entrapment may also interact with estrogen to trigger depression in adolescents. The term "entrapment" is used in the sense of an authority coercing someone to commit a crime or action that he or she would not otherwise have committed. There are many sources of entrapment in adolescence. Teenagers may feel compelled to act in a certain way to preserve friendships or social status. The pressure to commit even minor crimes or acts of truancy in order to garner social acceptance comes to mind. Some may feel entrapped by parents or grandparents regarding church attendance during periods of typical adolescent stages of questioning faith. These occasions of entrapment rob teenagers of their sense of autonomy and self-determination, leaving them with feelings of helplessness, resentment, and depression.

Behavior as Detection

Even with knowledge about these symptoms, it is difficult to detect depression in teenagers. Much of the depression experienced by adolescent women remains undetected and unreported, perhaps because many teenagers are confused by their feelings and wonder how talking about those feelings might impact their social identity. Many adolescent women may also be unaware that depression can be a common response to the natural change in the estrogen levels of their bodies. Instead, they may see their depression as a source of division or separation rather than an experience that could be shared. This attitude about depression can easily become another way of keeping young women isolated from their peers. As a result, many symptoms of adolescent depression are not specifically mentioned but are, instead, most easily observed and best detected in altered behavior, such as the following:

- **Pervasive sadness** may be represented by wearing black clothes, writing poetry with morbid themes, or preoccupation with music that has nihilistic themes.
- **Sleep disturbance** may manifest as watching television all night, difficulty getting up for school, or sleeping during the day.
- **Poor motivation and low energy** may be reflected by missed classes.
- **Social withdrawal** may be expressed by a reduction in social activities or loss of contact with friends.
- **Loss of concentration and slowed thinking** may be represented by a drop in grades or the inability to focus and complete homework.
- **Depressed thoughts** may be expressed as boredom by a teenager.

In short, adolescents communicate their depression through their behavior. This increases the need for parents, teachers, and professionals to be more vigilant in listening to the messages that are not being explicitly spoken.

SUICIDE

There is also a high risk for suicide among adolescents. Currently, suicide is the third leading cause of death among young adults between the ages of fifteen and twenty-four (Hauenstein 2003), and the rates have tripled over the past thirty years. This is largely due to a combination of increased stressors, which can include monthly surges in estrogen, and decreased resources available for dealing with depression in adolescence. Teenagers generally make more suicide attempts than adults, although they are also less successful in their attempts. Girls are significantly more likely to attempt suicide than boys but also to use methods that are likely to lead to revival, such as overdosing on sleeping pills. Boys are five times more likely to actually commit or complete suicide because they use techniques that lead to instant death, such as firearms or hanging.

When trying to detect suicidal tendencies, note that suicide is most likely to occur in two types of adolescents: high achievers and those who act out.

High achievement. High achievers are teenagers who are highly intelligent but who are solitary, withdrawn, and unable to meet their own expectations or the expectations of important figures in their lives. These are the boys and girls who perform well academically and receive As and Bs in school, but who are never satisfied with their performance. They feel isolated from others because their high internal and external demands make them feel inadequate and separate from others.

One of our previous clients, Elizabeth, was a teenage girl struggling with intense levels of depression. The interesting thing was that she received an exceptional amount of praise. Many teenagers receive little to no positive reinforcement and grow up believing their actions have little effect on others. But she started seeing herself as distinct and set apart from others. Because she kept receiving praise for her performance, she always felt inadequate, as if her self-worth was somehow linked with her achievement. This made her feel as though she consistently needed to improve her performance or fill higher expectations to elicit others' love and approval. In a sense, she thought that she was fundamentally flawed, that she always needed to correct a part of herself, and that she could never achieve contentment. Teachers consistently praised her drawings and told her that she was special, but she learned to feel that she was "too special." She became so special that she was somehow different from others, as if she was on the outside looking in, wanting simply to be ordinary. One irony was that every single drawing she made, the very thing that was helping to keep her feeling special and isolated, was a picture of two people, walking hand in hand down a road or on a beach. At the core, she simply wanted to be connected to, not separated from, others and their expectations. When her sense of loneliness was coupled with her changing estrogen levels, she began experiencing a high level of depression that included thoughts of suicide.

Acting out. The second type of adolescent at risk for suicide is the boy or girl who converts their depression to an outward expression, in the form of antisocial tendencies. These are the teenagers who express their depression through bullying, fighting, stealing, and increased risk taking and drug use. These are the teenagers who cry out for someone to alleviate their pain, almost to the point that they are willing to inflict this pain on others so that their anguish is shared or that their own pain is minimized. At the heart of these teenagers are strong feelings of despair, loneliness, and hopelessness. These methods of acting out should be seen as signs of underlying depression and indicators of risks for suicide.

Depression in Girls

When it comes to adolescent boys and girls, it is probably safe to say that the commonalities in the symptoms of depression are stronger than the differences. At the same time, it is important to recognize that depression may have a slightly different face in girls. For example, depression in girls is much more likely to be governed by feelings of worthlessness and guilt (Bennett et al. 2005). There is a strong tendency for girls to engage in more self-evaluation and self-criticism than boys. Some of this may be due to greater levels of concern about physical image, as well as the perceived expectation to suppress their autonomy and control. The greater emphasis on boys to be creative, take risks, and express their feelings behaviorally may account for their greater tendency to have problems with anger and high-risk behaviors. In contrast, girls' concerns about external image and suppression of power may engender feelings of worthlessness, just as guilt can be born from their concern about the impact of their actions on others.

One of the by-products of this is that girls are also more likely to experience *somatic*, that is, physical symptoms as part of their depression (Egger et al. 1999; Marcus et al. 2005). They are more inclined to have headaches, nausea, fatigue, and weight gain than boys, perhaps because their concerns about physical image and the pressure to restrict "acting out" behaviors naturally lead to a physical expression of depression. Boys have less restriction regarding agitation and irritability. Acting out may give them greater freedom to express their underlying feelings of sadness. But girls are more likely to focus on the internal process of their feelings, resulting in mental and physical pains.

Aidan and Anna present a strong example of this. These teenage siblings were brought to family therapy because of their parents' recent divorce. One of the first things that struck us was that they were both depressed but in distinctly different ways. Aidan had some underlying feelings of insecurity, but he expressed them through anger, irritation, and sneaking out at night. Anna was also depressed, and her depression was made worse by the onset of puberty, but she expressed it through crying and having an upset stomach. Through therapy, we were able to determine that both Aidan and Anna were troubled about their parents' divorce. They were confused about the new living arrangements and missed each parent on alternating weekends. However, their reactions to these feelings were very different. Aidan thought he could get his parents to join together in response if he acted out, which represented a way to unite them, even if it was against him. Anna felt ignored, confused about her changing body, and responded by weeping in private. Both adolescents struggled with understandable depression, but each responded or expressed their depression in distinct ways.

Searching for Answers & Help

Unfortunately, not much attention is devoted to the depression that is experienced by many adolescent women. Many adolescents and their doctors brush off depression as a natural phase of development. Teenage girls may leave doctors' offices feeling like depression is just a natural part of pubertal changes that should simply be endured. This may be why only 20 percent of depressed adolescents typically receive treatment (Martin and Cohen 2000).

To date, there is no accepted medication for adolescent depression. Many drug companies find it difficult to manufacture medications that are sensitive to the changing biological systems of adolescents. Many medications also require a relatively stable and predictable internal environment to maintain their effectiveness. The brains and bodies of teenagers are in such a constant state of change that they limit the value and elevate the risk of existing antidepressant interventions.

This has led to some recent controversy about the safety and efficacy of using antidepressants in adolescence. The regulatory agencies in the United States, the United Kingdom, and Canada have each issued warnings about the increased risk of suicidal behavior in adolescents using antidepressants. The difficulty in interpreting this increased risk, however, is that suicide attempts and suicidal ideation are themselves common symptoms of depression. If a suicide attempt is made during the course of treatment, it is difficult to identify the cause or causes of the event. It may be due to the antidepressant medication, or it could be due to a lack of improvement or a worsening of depressive symptoms. Considering the potential benefit from medications, as well as the ambiguity about the relationship between medications and suicide risk, it is unlikely that drug therapy will be abandoned as a potential form of treatment of depression in adolescents.

Whether or not teenagers are being treated with medication, we should not lower our vigilance regarding their depression. Questions about mood, behavior, and other symptoms of depression should be asked on a regular basis. Medical and psychological professionals have self-report inventories and screening methods that can identify depression at multiple levels. Psychotherapy has proven useful for alleviating depression in adolescents. It may take some time for a teenager to begin trusting a stranger, even if he or she is a professional, so therapy can require a lot of patience and understanding. However, it has helped provide adolescents with social-skills training, relaxation and coping strategies, and ways to replace negative thoughts and relationships with more adaptive ones.

Conclusion

Puberty is a difficult time for almost everyone. Each of us has our own battle wounds from this phase of personal development. For many of us, the emotional and physical scars can run deep. It is the one time in life that most of us would not want to relive. When talking with family or friends, very seldom will you hear fond memories of adolescence. We remember the childhood years before puberty with warmth, and we may pine for the days of college and our thirties, but the stories about puberty are different. They are stories of confusion, rebellion, and maybe even humiliation and shame. Granted, there are rousing moments of victory and tender moments of intimacy interspersed amidst the pain, but we often wish we could go back and offer solace and direction to that younger and wandering part of ourselves.

For women, the difficulty of puberty is often made worse because this may be the first time they have had to grapple with depression. Not all adolescent girls become depressed, but the rates of depression rise sharply for girls during the middle of puberty. One of the key factors contributing to this rise is the fluctuation in estrogen associated with puberty. Some depression may constitute emotional reactions to these physical changes, but the rise and fall of estrogen is one of the primary culprits in adolescent depression. This fluctuation seems to potentiate the risk for depression in certain, but not all, adolescent women (Angold et al. 1999). Put differently, the estrogen changes at puberty may exceed a threshold at which some adolescent women are susceptible to depression. Clearly, puberty represents the beginning of a developmental pathway of depression that is linked to surges in estrogen and that will extend throughout a woman's life. One of our primary goals is to help adolescent girls realize that they do not suffer alone. Women, in particular, share a common link to depression—their changing estrogen levels. As we will see in the coming chapters, this link is maintained throughout the female life span, whenever changes in estrogen levels occur.

CHAPTER 3

Premenstrual Syndrome & Premenstrual Dysphoric Disorder

"Dr. Henderson, I'm just not sure what I should do."

Dr. Henderson looked up from the notes she was making for Lisa's physical. "What do you mean?"

"This is so hard for me to talk about." Lisa looked down, swinging her legs a bit off the edge of the examination table, and took a deep breath. "I think I need something to help my mood."

Dr. Henderson put her pen down. "Can you tell me a little about it?"

"Everything just feels so uncontrollable right now. I've noticed this before—it seems to happen right before my menstrual cycle. I just feel so irritable, moody, and depressed."

Lisa paused, trying to pick her words carefully. She liked Dr. Henderson but still found it difficult to talk with her about this. She continued, "Just last night I blew up at my husband. With Michelle, our youngest, having problems in school, and with the opportunity to get promoted to manager in my job, we just haven't had any time to ourselves, let alone together. So we were looking forward to going out to a nice, relaxing dinner. It started out well. We had a pleasant ride over to the restaurant in the car, with each of us sharing about how our days had gone. Andy even let me choose the restaurant, which was a quaint little Italian place where we got a table in the corner by the fireplace. But that's when things deteriorated. The waitress brought out the wrong wine for me, and then I got irate when she mixed up my order. I can't explain it; I just lost control. I yelled at the waitress, picked up my plate, and slammed it down on the table and, in the process, knocked over my wine, spilling it onto my favorite outfit. Andy tried to calm me down, but I snapped at him. That's when I broke down crying. I told Andy I just wanted to go home, so we left the restaurant without ever eating.

"And that's not the only thing that's happened. The other night I got so mad at Andy that I threw a carton of milk at him; it hit the wall and got all over the floor. He hadn't done anything horrible, but I wasn't able to control my reactions. They just flare up like that. And I'm scared because I don't know if I can control myself at work. If I take this new position, I'm going to be the sales executive for our pharmaceutical company, which means that I have to be even tempered, alert, and collected. What if I lose it with a potential customer? Or worse yet, what if I lose it with Michelle?

"I know about PMS. I know many of these symptoms are related to PMS. I talked to my mom about it, and she was understanding, up to a point, but she basically said that I just need to deal with it, that it's simply a part of being a woman. I don't think I can do this alone. I'm scared, frustrated, and feel defeated by my own body. I don't know what to do."

Sound Familiar?

This is not an uncommon experience among women. Time after time, in our private practices, we hear stories from women about changes in mood and physical health that precede their menstrual cycle. They tell us about feelings of irritability, depression, rapid fluctuations in mood, decreased sexual interest, and a loss of excitement about things they previously enjoyed. Alone, these emotional changes are difficult to handle, but they are often coupled with physical changes that include bloating and breast tenderness. It is this pattern of symptoms, occurring during the week prior to menses and ending right after menses, that make up the conditions known as *premenstrual syndrome* (PMS) and the more severe *premenstrual dysphoric disorder* (PMDD). These syndromes represent the next stage or phase when estrogen can have a direct impact on the mood of women, making it important to understand PMS and PMDD, and how their symptoms of depression are linked to changes in estrogen levels.

The reality that PMS exists has been well established. In fact, Hippocrates, one of the forefathers of medicine, was among the first to describe a "tempestuous premenstrual syndrome," which he attributed to agitated blood that was seeking to escape from the womb. In their writings, authors from the Renaissance period made references to mood swings during the premenstrual phase, but PMS did not become a medically or popularly recognized phenomenon until the nineteenth century, when terms like "menstrual madness" and "ovarian mania" were linked to the function of the ovaries. It became fashionable between 1870 and 1900 to control premenstrual symptoms by removing both ovaries in a procedure known as a bilateral oopherectomy. However, it was not until the 1930s, and especially in the 1950s, that the term "premenstrual syndrome" came into fashion and that the full range of emotional and physical symptoms that we associate with it were recognized.

What Is PMS?

Since PMS is a condition that is directly related to the menstrual cycle, it may be helpful to quickly review the stages of that cycle.

The Menstrual Cycle

The *menstrual cycle* occurs about every twenty-eight days and generally refers to the process by which the body of a sexually mature woman releases an egg and prepares for the implantation of a fertilized egg to establish pregnancy. This process generally occurs in four phases:

1. **Menstruation.** In this phase, the lining of the uterus is shed. The release of this lining and the associated blood products are commonly referred to as a woman's *period* or *menses*. This phase is often thought to mark the beginning of the menstrual cycle because it represents the beginning of a new attempt for the female body to achieve pregnancy. It lasts anywhere from two to seven days, with an average length of three to five days.

2. **Follicular phase.** Following menstruation, a hormone in the woman's body called the *hypothalamic gonadotropin releasing hormone* (GnRH) stimulates the anterior pituitary gland to release a *follicle stimulating hormone* (FSH). The role of FSH is to stimulate the growth of *follicles*, or sacks, where a developing egg can grow. This phase typically begins around day seven and ends around day thirteen.

3. **Ovulation.** When the follicle has matured, it secretes enough estrogen to trigger the release of *luteinizing hormone* (LH), which serves to mature and release the egg (in a process called *ovulation*). This process lasts approximately two days, typically around days fourteen and fifteen of the menstrual cycle.

4. **Luteal phase.** During this phase, FSH and LH promote the formation of the *corpus luteum*, which is the solid body that forms after the residual follicle has released the egg. The corpus luteum produces progesterone and estrogen, which initiate the formation of a new layer of lining in the uterus where a fertilized embryo can implant itself. If pregnancy has not occurred, the corpus luteum dies, and progesterone levels fall. This progesterone withdrawal leads to menstrual shedding and the beginning of a new cycle. In total, the luteal phase generally begins around day sixteen and ends around day twenty-eight.

Where Does PMS Fit In?

PMS refers to the emotional and physical symptoms that occur during the last phase of the menstrual cycle—the luteal phase. It typically occurs after ovulation (that is, the release of the egg) or two weeks prior to the onset of menstruation and menstrual bleeding—hence the term, *premenstrual syndrome*. The symptoms of PMS disappear shortly after menstrual bleeding begins.

For most women, PMS symptoms first appear between the ages of twenty-five and thirty-five. Over three hundred symptoms have been associated with PMS, although there are twenty or so core symptoms (Halbreich 2003; Landen and Eriksson 2003). The most common symptoms can be broken down into emotional, behavioral, and physical categories, as shown in table 3.1.

TABLE 3.1: CORE SYMPTOMS OF PMS

Emotional Symptoms	Behavioral Symptoms	Physical Symptoms
Irritability	Fatigue	Abdominal bloating
Depression	Insomnia	Headaches
Anxiety	Dizziness	Breast tenderness
Impulsivity	Decreased sexual interest	Swelling of extremities
Mood swings	Increased appetite	Joint pain
Reduced self-esteem		Cramps

The difficulty with identifying these as PMS symptoms, however, is that they can also be explained by other factors. Granted, the regular appearance of these symptoms prior to menstruation makes it easy to assume that they are associated with the menstrual cycle, but other disorders or conditions must be ruled out before diagnosing these as PMS symptoms (Dickerson, Mazyck, and Hunter 2003). Anorexia, anemia, hypothyroidism, substance abuse, and some personality disorders can all show symptoms similar to PMS. This makes it necessary for physicians and clinicians to carefully monitor and determine the exact cause of individual symptoms to ensure that the best treatment is provided.

To help distinguish PMS from other syndromes, the American College of Obstetricians and Gynecologists created a set of criteria for diagnosing PMS (ACOG 2000). Their final conclusion was that PMS can be diagnosed when the following conditions are present:

- A woman reports one or more of the following emotional and physical symptoms during the five days before menses in three consecutive menstrual cycles:
  - Depression
  - Abdominal bloating
  - Angry outbursts
  - Headaches
  - Irritability

- Breast tenderness

- Anxiety

- Swelling of extremities

- Confusion

- Social withdrawal

- The symptoms must be relieved within four days of the onset of menstruation, without reappearing until at least thirteen days after the beginning of a new menstrual cycle.

- The symptoms must not be due to medications, the effect of ingested hormones, or drug or alcohol abuse.

- Based on records in a daily diary, the symptoms must occur regularly during two consecutive menstrual cycles.

- The symptoms must interfere with social, occupational, or educational functioning.

This suggests that a diagnosis of PMS can be clearly made when a woman experiences emotional and/or physical symptoms that are cyclical, occur during the luteal phase, cause significant concern, and cannot be attributed to another condition. Up to 95 percent of women with regular menstrual cycles meet these criteria and have some form of PMS (Backstrom et al. 2003; Steiner, Dunn, and Born 2003).

And the prevalence of this condition appears to be cross-cultural. Although some researchers have suggested that PMS merely represents a Western construct, recent cross-cultural reviews of emotional and physical symptoms show that symptoms of PMS appear to persist with equal rates in Europe, the United States, and non-Western cultures (Eriksson et al. 2002). This highlights the prevalence and cross-cultural consistency of this condition, as well as the strong burden it imposes on psychological and physical well-being.

PMS: Normal Event or Medical Condition?

This high prevalence has led many clinicians and researchers to wonder if PMS can truly be considered a medical condition or if it simply reflects a normal phenomenon. If we say that it is a disease or distinct medical condition, then we have pathologized what appear to be common emotional and physical symptoms among women. This can lead many women to feel as if their premenstrual experiences are somehow wrong or reflect a flaw in them. On the other hand, if we say that PMS is simply a common phenomenon and not a disease state, we risk trivializing the more serious symptoms of this condition. This commonly occurs when doctors or, perhaps, older women suggest that the symptoms of PMS are simply part of being a woman. Unfortunately, this may lead some women to sit silently in their anguish and feel helpless to control or reduce their symptoms, resulting in an underpursuit of treatment or an underadministration of effective treatments.

As a case in point, a client of ours, Angela, has extremely severe premenstrual symptoms. She experiences intense migraines, extreme mood fluctuations, and cramping that causes her to double over in pain. The pain associated with the cramping occasionally becomes so intense and severe that she loses consciousness and experiences seizures. As a result, she has to spend much of her premenstrual phase at home in bed, which interferes with her work and relationships. However, her family has become so desensitized and immune to these experiences that when she doubles over in pain or becomes agitated, they say, "Oh, it's just Angela's time of the month."

This sounds heartless, but it is probably a common experience among many women whose symptoms may be less severe than Angela's. This response minimizes the pain and trivializes the depression that many women experience during the premenstrual phase. It also means that we overlook the large burdens that may come along with depression and the other symptoms of PMS, such as lost quality of life and significant social and economic consequences. Therefore, it is important to note that while a certain number of depressive symptoms of PMS are normal in the premenstrual phase of the menstrual cycle, these symptoms are still worthy of treatment, especially among those women whose depressive symptoms can be severe and debilitating.

Depression, PMS & PMDD

Where does depression fit into PMS and PMDD? The symptoms of depression, including irritability and sadness, are the most common features of PMS. Some are relieved when they hear this because it validates and normalizes their experience. Others are surprised by this, or find it a provocative contention, because they find it difficult to believe that mood can be so intimately connected with their menstrual cycles. But if they think back on their own experiences and those of their friends, they may find that mood changes are highly prevalent during PMS.

One of the women we spoke to put it this way:

It is almost as if women and men alike carry around a dualistic perception of ourselves. We somehow split the mind from the body. We think of depression as a condition of the mind but [of] menstruation as a condition of the body. Maybe we do this because we like to see ourselves as being able to control the mind, as if depression and other emotional symptoms are within our own power. We relegate menstruation and the menstrual cycle to the body, but this is somehow more acceptable because they are products beyond our control. But this means that we are less inclined to think of depression as a feature of PMS because we are less willing to think of it as something that the body has control over and that might be beyond our control.

This line of thinking may help explain some of the reluctance to attribute depression to PMS. It may be easier for some women to accept physical symptoms such as bloating, body tenderness, and headaches, rather than depression, as symptoms of PMS. Maybe depression seems more psychological than biological, and therefore we think that it's more within our conscious control than are these physical symptoms. This reasoning is supported by older theories that PMS, particularly depression in the context of PMS, is a cognitive or social creation, lacking scientific evidence of its existence.

But the reality is that a woman's mood during PMS and PMDD cannot be disconnected from the biological changes that are occurring during the luteal phase of the menstrual cycle. If we were to plot the course of the mood of a woman with PMS onto the course of her menstrual cycle, the emerging picture would show depression peaking a few days before the onset of menstruation and rapidly disappearing once bleeding begins (Metcalf and Livesey

1995). This is the time when estrogen levels are at their lowest. The moods of women with PMS are most positive somewhere between the end of menstrual bleeding and the early luteal phase, when estrogen levels are highest. This suggests that a woman's mood can be significantly influenced by her menstrual cycle. In fact, 46 percent of those admitted to psychiatric hospitals for depression are admitted at, or immediately prior to, menstruation (Payne 2003). Not only that, but the risk for suicide in women is highest during this time. This makes it hard to argue that depression and PMS are purely mentally or socially constructed events.

Premenstrual Dysphoric Disorder

For approximately 2 to 8 percent of women, these symptoms of depression become so severe and debilitating that they meet full criteria for a condition known as *premenstrual dysphoric disorder* (PMDD) (Dickerson, Mazyck, and Hunter 2003; Downey 1999). This condition was recently included as a form of "depressive disorder not otherwise specified" in the *Diagnostic and Statistical Manual of Mental Disorders* (DSM-IV) (APA 1994), which is the hallmark manual for psychological conditions. To meet criteria for this condition, the following must be present:

- A woman must report five or more of the following symptoms:
    - Markedly depressed mood
    - Lack of energy
    - Marked anxiety
    - Change in appetite
    - Mood swings
    - Feeling out of control
    - Marked anger or irritability
    - Other physical symptoms
    - Decreased interest in usual activities
    - Difficulty concentrating

- The symptoms must be present most of the time during the last week of the luteal phase and stop within a few days after the onset of the follicular phase.

- The symptoms must interfere with work, school, or usual social activities and relationships.

- The symptoms cannot represent the worsening of another disorder, such as panic disorder or a personality disorder.

- These symptoms must be confirmed in at least two consecutive symptomatic cycles.

This means that women with PMDD experience distinct mood symptoms, their symptoms interfere with regular activities, they have no symptoms in the follicular phase, and they have confirmed the presence of these symptoms for at least two menstrual cycles. As with PMS, the onset of PMDD occurs during the teens to late twenties, with the symptoms peaking in the thirties and early forties (Desai and Jann 2000). In essence, PMDD is a severe form of PMS that is not only characterized by physical symptoms, but also by emotional concerns that are severe enough to interfere with work, school, and relationships.

This does not suggest that physical symptoms are absent. Quite the contrary: most women with PMDD experience the breast tenderness, bloating, and headaches associated with PMS. But they also experience strong levels of depression that are incapacitating and interfere with their daily lives. For most of those with PMDD, the change in the severity of their moods is striking. During the luteal phase, there is typically a 30 to 50 percent increase in symptom severity (Ross and Steiner 2003), which returns to normal levels in the follicular phase. If you are one of the women who experience these dramatic shifts in mood, your life is transformed each month. Women who are typically optimistic and even-keeled can become pessimistic and irritable. Even those who are the most attentive and diligent at work and have high levels of work productivity can struggle to remain focused and efficient. Energy levels may drop, anxiety may increase, and hope can be abandoned.

Kathy represents a good example of this. She dreads menstruation not only because of the physical discomfort it causes, but also because she becomes extremely depressed during the week prior to her period. She becomes easily tearful watching commercials and movies, struggles to get out of bed and shower in the morning, and becomes irritable with the slightest provocation. In his attempt to be humorous, her husband has labeled her Dr. Jekyll and Mrs. Hyde; these names hurt, but she recognizes the truth behind them.

During one of her sessions with us, she related a story of how she was trying to leave the house to get to work during one of her premenstrual weeks. She was running behind schedule because it was hard for her to get up and her new puppy was refusing to get in its kennel. Trying to be playful, the puppy ran under a desk and hid in the shadows, just out of Kathy's reach. She was trying to talk it out of its hiding place, but she became so frustrated after a couple of minutes that she broke into tears and started swearing at the dog. She picked up a pencil and threw it under the desk, hoping it would scare the dog enough to come out. Instead, it struck the dog in its eye, causing the eye to bleed. The puppy whimpered and came out, still wagging its tail, hoping to play. After seeing the bloody eye, Kathy just sat on the ground and cried, feeling horrible about herself. She was plagued with so much guilt that she called her husband, asking him to take the dog away. She even found herself wondering if she should go on living. Even though she knew logically that she was overreacting to what had happened, her thoughts about suicide represented a way to escape her depression and guilt. Kathy's experience would meet the criteria for PMDD, and it attests to the intense emotional sensitivity that can occur for women with PMDD. Her experience also reveals the despair and hopelessness that many women feel, as well as the power this condition can have over women's lives.

Symptoms of Depression in PMS & PMDD

Clearly, both PMS and PMDD have a negative impact on a woman's emotional health. PMDD is itself a disorder of depression, and PMS is clearly implicated in the depression that women may experience monthly. The question is, What does this depression look like for most women with PMS and PMDD?

IRRITABILITY

Irritability is by far the most common symptom of depression during PMS and PMDD. Most women with PMS report some level of irritability, and up to 97 percent of women with PMDD report high levels of irritability, with most of this occurring during the luteal phase (Landen and Eriksson 2003). When researchers plotted this irritability onto the course of the menstrual cycle, they discovered that the severity of women's irritability increased during the luteal phase and peaked during the last five premenstrual days or the first day of menstruation. After a few days of menstrual bleeding, the symptoms completely disappeared (Backstrom et al. 2003). This may explain the sudden outbursts, increased feelings of aggression, and elevated sensitivity to the statements or actions of others that many women may feel in the premenstrual stages.

Irritability is not only the most common, but it is also the most behaviorally obvious symptom of depression during PMS and PMDD, primarily because it is difficult to hide. Many women may discipline their emotions during the rest of their menstrual cycle, but the week prior to menstruation finds them sighing in response to others' complaints, snapping at others' failures, or becoming easily frustrated with themselves. They may become slightly more aggressive (for example, while driving), give up more quickly and angrily (say, slamming doors when they cannot find something), and speak more curtly (for example, when a cashier is slow). One of our clients even told us that she noticed a change in her e-mails during her luteal phase. Most of the time, her e-mails were thoughtful and professional responses, but during the premenstrual phase, she noticed that her messages were shorter, more terse, and bordered on being both defensive and angry. The irritability associated with PMS can manifest itself in many forms.

Irritability can be frightening to women who may be scared of their inability to control themselves. They often come to our offices or the offices of their physicians concerned about their outbursts, concerned about whether these outbursts will be directed at their children. They recognize that irritability can lead to interpersonal conflicts, making them more susceptible to hurting their relationships and to acting in ways that can be drastically different from their normal patterns. Like most individuals, these women also see their irritability as somehow tied to their personalities or their dispositions. Since

48

irritability has a behavioral component and is typically expressed in outward form, these women are afraid that these outbursts define them as irritable and uncontrollable people. The reality is that they are simply women with PMS. Addressing the stigma associated with irritability calls for greater sensitivity to PMS and the frequent irritability that accompanies it.

SADNESS

Sadness is the next most common symptom of depression in PMS and PMDD. It occurs in 90 percent of women with either condition, and, as with irritability, the severity of sadness increases during the luteal phase and peaks during the last five premenstrual days or the first day of menstruation (Backstrom et al. 2003). Unlike irritability, however, sadness can be an internalized symptom; for example, many women may cry without fully knowing the reason why. Often, this sadness is made worse by the feelings of low self-esteem, guilt, and self-doubt that can also accompany PMS and PMDD. Women in this emotional state can become easily overwhelmed and lack interest in previously pleasant activities, like exercise, reading, or personal hobbies. They may lack motivation, feel powerless, want to sleep more than usual, and in severe cases, may contemplate suicide. Ironically, this sadness can lead to social withdrawal and increase their sense of isolation and loneliness. And when they are with others, this sadness may make them quiet and reserved, which frequently intensifies their depression.

LACK OF SEXUAL INTEREST

There are a host of other depressive symptoms associated with PMS and PMDD. Anxiety and tension are common as well as restlessness and loneliness. There is also an overall lowering of sexual interest in the luteal and premenstrual phases (Dennerstein et al. 1994). The return of sexual interest appears to occur during the follicular and ovulatory phases, which suggests that sexual appetite is somehow directly linked to the changes occurring in the menstrual cycle. This may be the result of the body's evolutionary adaptation. During the follicular phase, when the woman's body is primed for the implantation of a fertilized egg in the uterus, an increase in sexual interest enhances the possibility for pregnancy. The sudden and sharp drop in sexual interest after ovulation coincides with the reduced likelihood for fertilization.

Although this process may reflect the result of evolutionary processes aimed at sustaining the human species, it is also significant that this drop in sexual interest occurs alongside the increase in other symptoms of depression, including sadness and irritability. When you feel depressed and irritable, sex is less likely to be on your mind. While the changes in sexual appetite associated with PMS and PMDD are probably part of the body's way of maximizing fertilization, they are also a symptom of depression and may additionally be a response to the sadness and irritability that emerge during the premenstrual period.

Risk Factors for PMS or PMDD

There is a subset of conditions that may elevate a woman's risk for developing depression during the luteal phase. As with estrogen fluctuation during puberty, the change in hormonal environment during the luteal phase makes women more susceptible to depression. For some women, the simple fluctuation in estrogen during this phase is sufficient to lead to depression. For others, it is the combined action of estrogen fluctuation and these additional risk factors that turns depression from a possibility into a reality.

GENETICS

Among these additional risk factors is a strong genetic inheritance of depressive symptoms in PMS. In a study of 5,000 pairs of mothers and adolescent daughters, there was a strong correlation between the PMS symptoms experienced by both. If the mother had symptoms of irritability and depression, 70 percent of the daughters had similar symptoms, but if the mothers were relatively symptom free during the premenstrual phase, 63 percent of the daughters were also symptom free (Halbreich 2003; Widholm and Kantero 1971). This suggests that the daughters of women afflicted with depression during PMS have compounded risk for developing depression during their own menstrual cycles.

Similarly, a study of 1,312 twins showed that identical twins were twice as likely to have similar premenstrual symptoms, including depression, than fraternal twins (Kendler et al. 1992, 1998). Other twin studies have shown that approximately 56 percent of premenstrual symptoms can be traced to genetic factors (Ross and Steiner 2003). This does not explain the exact mechanics of PMS and depression in the female body, but it suggests that the closer two women are in genetic structure, the more likely they are to experience similar depressive symptoms during PMS.

It is uncertain which genes are actually involved in PMS and its symptoms of depression. The most likely candidates include those genes that are important in forming estrogen and other hormones, primarily because these hormones are so integral to the menstrual cycle and the symptoms of PMS (Eriksson et al. 2002). Regardless of the specific genes, however, it is important to note that the depressive symptoms associated with PMS and PMDD can be partially influenced by genetic factors.

HISTORY OF DEPRESSION

Women are also more likely to develop PMDD and depression in PMS if they have a prior history of depression. Some of the more recent findings suggest that 30 to 80 percent of women who have a history of major depression are likely to develop PMDD (Halbreich 2003; Payne 2003). Even those who had only a few symptoms of depression unrelated to PMS and for less than two weeks were at increased risk for future episodes of depression, including sadness and irritability, during PMS (Halbreich 2003).

These women might have an increased vulnerability to mood symptoms during PMS. In the same way that genetics can leave the brain more primed to develop depression during PMS, an earlier experience of depression can lower the threshold for developing future depression, especially when the hormonal environment is weakened by estrogen's ebb and flow. These early experiences can change the brain's biochemistry, including the sensitivity to various neurotransmitters, which can render some women more predisposed to developing depressive symptoms in response to stress and other bodily changes, such as PMS. For example, 40 percent of women with PMS, including symptoms of depression, also have a history of sexual abuse or of significantly stressful life events (Ross and Steiner 2003). These early events can have lasting and pervasive effects on the psychological and biological development of women, particularly in terms of a woman's response to future stressors like PMS. Taken together, a woman's genetic makeup, prior history of depression, and exposure to stressful life events appear to create a heightened vulnerability or sensitivity to the changes associated with PMS, making her more susceptible to depression. But what are the biological mechanisms that lead to the emergence of depression in PMS and PMDD?

Why Depression Develops in PMS & PMDD

Of the four key occasions of hormonal fluctuation in a woman's life—puberty, PMS, postpartum depression, and the phases of menopause—PMS may reveal the clearest connection between estrogen and depression. The fact that the symptoms of PMS and PMDD appear only during a certain phase of the menstrual cycle suggests that these symptoms are associated with the fluctuating hormones involved in the menstrual cycle. In particular, the fluctuation of estrogen and progesterone have been implicated as significant factors contributing to the symptoms of PMS. The development of mood changes and other symptoms of PMS appears to be closely connected to the rise and fall of estrogen and progesterone during the luteal, or premenstrual, phase of the menstrual cycle (Fink et al. 1996; Wieck 1996). Estrogen peaks prior to ovulation and drops sharply toward the end of the menstrual cycle, whereas progesterone peaks after ovulation and before the menses (Halbreich 2003). It is this rise in progesterone and withdrawal of estrogen that may account for some of the depressive symptoms emerging in PMS and PMDD.

If a woman were to keep a daily diary of her menstrual cycle and mood, she would likely find that her irritability and feelings of sadness increase during the luteal phase and peak during the last five days prior to menstruation. If we drew her blood and assessed her hormone levels at this point, we would find that her estrogen levels had dropped and her progesterone levels had increased. In a sense, the rise in irritability and depression parallels the rise in progesterone and decline in estrogen. When estrogen returns and progesterone drops, the mood of women improves. This suggests that the rise and fall of depressive symptoms, such as irritability or lack of sexual interest, is biologically linked to the activity of the hormones estrogen and progesterone.

Additional Evidence

This role of hormones in PMS is supported by the effectiveness of treatments aimed at reducing the symptoms of PMS. Sometimes the best way to understand a condition is to find effective treatments and work backward to understand why they work. This is how we've learned much of what's known about the role of hormones in PMS. For example, giving a woman high doses of estrogen during the luteal phase has reduced the depressive symptoms of PMS (Arpels 1996; Halbreich and Kahn 2001). This points to the changes in estrogen levels as a potential contributor to PMS-related depression.

There are also certain agents that can eliminate the luteal phase and symptoms of PMS altogether by slowing estrogen and progesterone activity. The primary agents are chemicals that stimulate the release of GnRH. You may recall from our discussion of the menstrual cycle, earlier in this chapter, that GnRH stimulates the growth of follicles where a developing egg can grow. It also facilitates the production of estrogen and progesterone. But, with the excessive release of GnRH, a woman's body becomes desensitized to its effects so that normal production of estrogen and progesterone is interrupted. This suppresses the normal function of the ovaries (that is, ovulation) and reduces both the physical and emotional symptoms of PMS (Mortola, Girton, and Fischer 1991; Rapkin 2003). If the interruption of estrogen and progesterone production reduces PMS, this highlights their role in the symptoms and origins of PMS.

Schmidt and his colleagues (1998) from the National Institute of Mental Health attempted to blend these approaches to illuminate the connection between hormonal variation and the depressive symptoms of PMS. They first suppressed the normal functioning of the ovaries and eliminated the luteal phase of the menstrual cycle using GnRH stimulants. Then they reintroduced estrogen and progesterone into the body, only to discover that the symptoms of PMS returned. This suggests that changes in estrogen and progesterone are critical to the onset of the symptoms of PMS, strengthening the idea that PMS is triggered by hormonally related events.

Sensitivity to Changes

It is important to note that PMS-related depression does not appear to emerge due to absolute differences in the level of these hormones. All women experience the rise of progesterone and fall of estrogen during the luteal phase. And all women have similar levels of estrogen and progesterone during the luteal phase, regardless of whether or not they have PMS. In other words, there is no difference in the actual level of estrogen or progesterone between women with PMS and those without it (Young and Korszun 2002).

This suggests that PMS-related depression is not simply the result of high progesterone and low estrogen. This depression is not a dysfunction of the hormone changes themselves, but rather an abnormal sensitivity to these changes. The normal hormonal fluctuations in estrogen and progesterone appear to trigger PMS and depressive symptoms in women who may be vulnerable to mood disorders. It is *sensitivity* to these changes in levels of estrogen and progesterone that may account for differences in mood during PMS (Joffe and Cohen 1998; Payne 2003). And the root for much of this sensitivity may reside in the female brain's response to serotonin.

PMS, Depression & Serotonin

Changes in estrogen levels don't directly explain the appearance of depression in PMS and PMDD, but the evidence suggests that these level changes indirectly influence mood through the serotonin system. During the premenstrual phase, many women with PMS and PMDD have serotonin dysfunction, that is, a distinct change from the serotonin activity during the other phases of the menstrual cycle. Specifically, they show reduced serotonin levels, reduced serotonin uptake, and a depletion of the building blocks that create serotonin (Payne 2003; Ross and Steiner 2003). This may account for the 60 to 70 percent success rate of *selective serotonin reuptake inhibitors* (SSRIs) in reversing the symptoms of PMS (Halbreich and Kahn 2001).

In a study of 180 women, Steiner and his colleagues (1995) demonstrated the superior role of Prozac, an SSRI, in reducing symptoms of depression, irritability, and anxiety as compared to a placebo. Interestingly, SSRIs like Prozac typically take two to three weeks to begin reducing the symptoms of depression, but they are able to work within hours or days of administration for women with PMS and PMDD (Eriksson et al. 2002; Landen and Eriksson 2003). This has not only led SSRIs to become the first-line treatment for depression in PMS and PMDD, but it also confirms the role of serotonin in the pathology of PMS and PMDD.

Moreover, SSRIs are particularly effective in countering the cardinal symptom of PMS—irritability. They naturally inhibit the aggression and irritability associated with the luteal phase of the menstrual cycle. This suggests that dysfunction in serotonin levels and activity underlie some of the primary features of PMS and PMDD. From chapter I, we know that serotonin functioning is influenced by estrogen fluctuations, so many of the changes in mood that accompany PMS and PMDD reflect the interaction between serotonin and estrogen levels. It is unlikely that this interaction completely explains the depressive symptoms of women with PMS or PMDD, but for some women, the fluctuations in estrogen and serotonin that occur in the luteal phase of the menstrual cycle may lead to a greater susceptibility to depression. In other words, the significant changes in estrogen that characterize the premenstrual phase may disrupt the balance of the serotonin system and result in depression and irritability for some women.

Conclusion

PMS remains a hot topic of debate. Due to its prevalence, few patients or clinicians would deny that it exists. Instead, the debate centers on the severity of the symptoms. Some individuals like to poke fun at the concept of PMS. They freely admit that there are specific physical and emotional symptoms associated with the premenstrual phase, but they wonder if the media and larger culture have somehow imposed an unnecessarily negative connotation on normal and neutral physical changes. Individuals with this mind-set sometimes think PMS is being used as a convenient scapegoat for unwanted feelings, destructive behavior, and lack of job productivity.

This mind-set sounds a bit harsh and is probably a reflection of the strong value that Western cultures have placed on emotional control and predictability. This attitude is actually relatively recent. As a case in point, it is probably not coincidental that PMS was first clearly defined in the 1930s, when women were entering the workforce. Many individuals, both men and women, may have been concerned about the way irritability and depression during the premenstrual phase could influence job productivity, particularly in positions that required emotional control. Despite the political correctness that largely governs our culture, some of these questions likely remain. For example, many individuals still wonder if women should assume positions of leadership, such as the presidency, considering the reactivity and sensitivity that can occur with PMS and PMDD.

As a result of this mind-set, PMS has gained a somewhat pejorative connotation in the larger culture. It is the frequent topic of television sitcoms, self-help books, and even political platforms that discuss the role of women in the workplace. The danger in this mind-set is that it can and has been used to justify denying women equal access to education and employment. The instability during women's reproductive cycles has been used to argue that women cannot tolerate advanced education or that they should not hold positions of leadership. This cultural pressure leads many women to believe that the symptoms of PMS are somehow abnormal and should be masked, that they simply need to take a deep breath and cope with it, and that they should be resigned to suffer, perhaps unnecessarily. It leads them to avoid seeking treatment and perhaps to buy into the idea that they are somehow flawed or weak because of their monthly irritability and depression. It also leads physicians and other clinicians to trivialize and overlook the depression in PMS.

Does this mean that we should simply ignore the possible impact of mood changes in PMS and PMDD? Quite the contrary. It is important that we improve our understanding of the mood fluctuations associated with these conditions, not only to affirm the experiences of women, but also to understand how to treat them. And it may be important to change or alter the meaning that many women and men ascribe to these conditions. Rather than seeing the depression and mood swings that occur in PMS as a source of shame or weakness, maybe it would be more appropriate to see them for what they are—a susceptibility to the changes in hormone levels associated with the premenstrual phase of the menstrual cycle. This is not a vulnerability to the actual changes in the levels of estrogen or progesterone themselves, but rather a susceptibility to the impact of these changes on mood, likely occurring through the serotonin system. This is part of the process of bringing PMS and PMDD out of the closet of shame and placing them in perspective. The battle to do this is an uphill one and requires confronting and educating those who deny the impact of PMS.

CHAPTER 4

Postnatal & Postpartum Depression

Ethan's toes stuck out from under the blanket. They were so incredibly small, with tiny toenails that looked like they were carefully placed by a master craftsman on the appendages of a porcelain doll. Emily slowly rubbed her fingers over the sole of his foot. The skin was soft and supple. There were no rough calluses of the weary traveler.

She looked up at his face. His arms were splayed out on either side, somewhat carelessly and comically set there, as if he'd just fallen backward and had let his arms fly up near his head, which was turned slightly to the side, with eyes closed. Soft, short breaths emerged from his mouth, leaving the faint whisper of condensation on the bars of his crib. His face was smooth and slightly pudgy but lacked the wrinkles or blemishes caused by worry, sadness, or loss. She pulled the blanket over his toes.

And she began to cry.

She was not certain what the tears were for. It was three weeks after the birth of her first child, and this was supposed to be one of the best moments of her life. She had waited until her career was in a stable position, their finances were in good shape, and she and her husband felt emotionally prepared for the introduction of a new member into their family. The pregnancy itself had gone relatively smoothly, save for the typical back pain, nausea, and physical discomfort. And the delivery itself was without significant complication. But ever since Ethan had been born, Emily could not help but feel sad.

She knew that some of it was likely due to sleep deprivation. Heck, she was only getting three to four hours of unbroken sleep each night. And she felt slightly more alone because her mom had just left after visiting for three weeks.

But she was also becoming more irritable with her husband, did not want to see any visitors or friends, lacked any semblance of appetite, and found it difficult to muster the energy she needed to even shower each morning.

The worst part of it was the feelings of guilt. Although she would never fully express it to others, she often felt indifferent about her child. It was not that she didn't love Ethan—quite the contrary. But she didn't feel as emotionally attached as she wanted to, and she lacked any sense of pleasure in her life. She did not share the happiness about the birth that everyone else seemed to be feeling. The difficulty was that she felt like she was being selfish because of her emotions and her indifference, but she could not simply turn them off. In her mind, she kept telling herself, "I must be a terrible mother," which only served to increase her feelings of worthlessness.

The Stigma of Postpartum Depression

These are some of the signs of postpartum depression. The symptoms of this syndrome can often be the least socially acceptable forms of depression. Mothers are surrounded with cards and balloons that say "Congratulations!" They are sent flowers and gifts that are intended to cultivate a festive and happy environment. Friends and family expect reassurances that "Mom and baby are doing well!" so it might come as a shock to them to discover that the new mother was tearful and depressed. Concern would be heartfelt and sincere, but there might also be an underlying bias, found in contemporary culture, against any emotion that departs from happiness or joy following childbirth. This bias might also alienate the millions of women who experience symptoms of depression following childbirth, leading them to feel like there is a fundamental flaw or defect in who they are.

This is changing, as was seen in the recent debate about postpartum depression between Tom Cruise and Brooke Shields. This debate centered around Brooke's emotions following the birth of her daughter Rowan. Tom did not deny the reality of postpartum depression, but he did question the value of antidepressant medications as a treatment for it. The resulting backlash against his comments rallied support and appreciation for the pain and anguish that many women experience after childbirth, and it gave people an opportunity to talk about postpartum depression.

Most medical and mental health professionals agree that postpartum depression is a legitimate condition. And it is hard to argue with the statistics. Between 10 and 22 percent of women experience depressive symptoms within the first six months after childbirth, with the majority experiencing symptoms within the first month. Depressive symptoms can persist for up to one year among 40 percent of those affected (Halbreich and Kahn 2001; Studd and Panay 2004). In other words, one in four of all mothers will experience symptoms of depression. The impact of this depression on the mother, infant, and family can be profound. In fact, postpartum mood disorders represent the most frequent form of maternal disease following delivery (Dennis and Stewart 2004). This makes it particularly important to understand postpartum depression and its close connection with the changes in estrogen that are occurring in the postnatal bodies of women.

Three Syndromes of Postpartum Depression

The level of severity of these emotional difficulties ranges from early maternity blues to fully developed psychosis, but many have found it helpful to group these difficulties within three syndromes of postpartum mood disorder: postpartum blues, postpartum depression, and postpartum psychosis.

Postpartum Blues

Postpartum blues, or "baby blues," is the most mild of the postpartum depression syndromes. This syndrome is also the most common, occurring in approximately 70 percent of women, although it can range from 26 to 85 percent (Downey 1999; Steiner, Dunn, and Born 2003). The most common symptoms are shown in table 4.1.

TABLE 4.1: POSTPARTUM BLUES SYMPTOMS

Emotional Symptoms	Behavioral Symptoms
Depressed mood	Fatigue
Fluctuations between elation and sadness	Insomnia
Irritability	Confusion
Tearfulness	Reduced appetite
Anxiety	

These symptoms typically begin within the first three days after childbirth, peak on the fifth day, and resolve without treatment by the twelfth day. Considering the self-limiting nature of these symptoms, they are largely considered to be transient, temporary, and insufficient to cause serious interference with the mother or infant's personal and social functioning. And because of the high prevalence of these blues in most women, they are largely considered to be a normal part of the process of childbirth and recovery.

However, women shouldn't dismiss the postpartum blues just because the symptoms are relatively common. The experience of crying without a particular reason, becoming irritable at minor statements from family members, or not finding pleasure in one's infant can be distressing for a mother and her family.

Alyssa, who was one of our patients, described it as a feeling of "faking it." Immediately after her baby was born, the only thing she wanted to do was sleep. She had become pregnant with her boyfriend, who had encouraged her to have an abortion, but she decided she wanted to raise the child. She ended her relationship with the boyfriend because she was uncomfortable with his negative influence on her life. Due to her limited finances, she was not able to attend Lamaze or parenting classes. She had perused a couple of birthing books, but they did not fully address the reality of postpartum blues. She admitted that she half expected the delivery to resemble those on television. She remembered watching sitcoms where the father or nurse lovingly places the newborn in the mother's arms and they all smile and remark on how small the baby's hands are.

But for her it was completely different.

Starting about the second or third day after the birth, she began to have difficulty sleeping, lost her appetite, and found herself confused because she was more interested in what was occurring on television than with her own child, who was rooming with her. She expressed deep interest, love, and affection toward the child, but deep down, she felt like she was faking it to appease the visitors, nurses, and even her mom and dad when they came to visit. Nothing really excited her, and she frequently cried when her dad asked how she was doing. For her, it felt like an act to show joy externally that did not match how she was feeling internally.

These symptoms subsided about seven days after the delivery, when she developed a strong emotional connection to her child. However, it was not until after we got her connected with a mother's support group, where mothers were able to talk candidly about their experiences and emotions, that she realized that she had been experiencing postpartum blues.

Granted, some level of exhaustion and depression is normal following childbirth. In comical fashion, another one of our patients recently captured it this way: "You can't have nine months of physical distress, food cravings, vomiting, and another person pushing against your bladder; have your body toy with you by creating false contractions and false hope; go through several hours of excruciating labor pain where the doctors offer drugs only when the pain reaches an ungodly level; and push a large child through a small opening in your body and not feel somewhat tired and depressed."

So a little fatigue and sadness is to be expected following childbirth. But just because these symptoms may be part of the natural process of recovery after childbirth does not mean that they should be underappreciated. The minimization of postpartum blues leads many women to underreport their symptoms to physicians. By doing so, many women do not receive the opportunity to hear that the prognosis for postpartum blues is good, with most symptoms resolving within two weeks. They also miss out on education about the condition and the opportunity to receive emotional support during the process.

Just because Michelangelo suffered an expected level of severe back pain after working on the Sistine Chapel does not mean he failed to get it treated.

In the same way, just because postpartum blues are common and perhaps a natural follow-up to childbirth does not mean that they should be disregarded or trivialized.

Postpartum Depression

For approximately one or two in ten women, motherhood begins with a more severe level of depression. This more severe level is what is typically understood as the syndrome of *postpartum depression* (PPD). This is the diagnosis when the symptoms of depression last beyond the second week after childbirth. And, with the exception that this condition has the unique timing of following childbirth, the profile of PPD is exactly the same as the criteria for a major depressive condition, as described in the *Diagnostic and Statistical Manual of Mental Disorders* (DSM-IV), the hallmark manual for psychological conditions (APA 1994).

The criteria for this condition are as follows:

- A woman must report five or more of the following symptoms:
  - Markedly depressed mood
  - Lack of energy
  - Decreased interest in usual activities
  - Feelings of worthlessness
  - Insomnia
  - Recurrent thoughts of death
  - Significant weight loss or gain
  - Difficulties concentrating
- The symptoms must occur within four weeks of delivery.
- The symptoms must interfere with work or school or usual social activities and relationships.
- The symptoms cannot be due to substance use or another medical condition.

- These symptoms must be confirmed in at least two consecutive symptomatic cycles.

This means that women with PPD experience distinct mood symptoms within four weeks of delivery that interfere with regular activities and work, school, and relationships. Between 10 and 22 percent of all women meet criteria for PPD in the weeks following delivery (Payne 2003; Steiner, Dunn, and Born 2003), and most of these symptoms resolve within three to six months. Clearly, PPD is a disorder of depression that resembles other depressive periods, but as we will see, the close linkage to the hormonal fluctuations associated with childbirth seems to emphasize certain symptoms.

EMOTIONAL FLUCTUATION

By far some of the most common symptoms of PPD are emotional variability, guilt, and agitation (Hendrick, Altshuler, and Suri 1998). Most women with PPD report some fluctuation in their mood, which can range from sadness and tearfulness to irritability and even moments of elation. At any given moment, mood can become contingent upon environment. A funny segment on television or a remark by a friend can elicit laughter and joy, but these feelings can quickly turn to tearfulness when disparaging thoughts enter a woman's mind or when she is alone. Women with PPD can become easily overwhelmed and lack interest in previously pleasant activities, like reading, eating certain foods, or practicing personal hobbies.

The difficult and confusing thing about these emotional fluctuations is how uncontrollable they are. Some psychologists liken it to being a passenger on a freight train, which can be barreling along on one track but then suddenly shift to another. The difficulty is that women do not feel like the conductors, but rather the passengers, subject to the whim of something beyond their control.

There may be subtle reasons for these emotional shifts that remain undetectable, such as certain phrases you hear or fleeting thoughts about your value. But these are not experiences that would typically elicit such drastic changes in mood. It is as if the emotional state of a woman with PPD is much more raw, sensitive, and vulnerable after childbirth, without the protective layering that would normally stabilize mood in the face of these emotional fluctuations.

This is what happened to Rose. Her emotions were pretty stable during the first couple of days following the birth of her new daughter, but she really struggled with the transition back home. On the one hand, she wanted her husband to be supportive, to help out and share some of the responsibilities for cooking, cleaning, and getting up in the night to care for their baby. And he responded well to this. In his enthusiasm and excitement about their new child, he kept asking if there was anything he could do to help or anything he could go out and get for her. But she noticed that she was becoming easily annoyed with him. It felt almost as if he was trying to buy her off or trying to establish a private bond with their child that excluded her. She knew this was not the case, but she found herself snapping at him more frequently. At other times, she broke into tears when he made dinner, simply because she realized how much he truly cared for her. She kept vacillating between these different emotions. At times, she felt like her emotions were out of control, and her husband began acting like a rat in a lion's cage, never certain which way to go or how she was going to respond.

GUILT

It is uncertain whether the guilt of the postpartum mother is a direct expression of depression or rather a reaction to it, but what remains clear is that many of the women with PPD feel guilty that their emotions do not match what they believe or hope they should be. For many women, there is a stark contrast between what they want to be feeling and the sadness and despondency they feel inside. The external world of these mothers is typically one of celebration, but while fathers and grandparents are sending out pictures, passing out cigars, and planning for baptisms or other religious events, mothers may be indifferent and tearful. Few mothers feel completely free to acknowledge these emotions due to the social stigma that is attached, but the reality is that they may be disinterested or have negative feelings about the child.

Dr. Jennifer Downey of the Columbia University College of Physicians and Surgeons related the following personal story:

I was in the hospital for five days after a cesarean section, and my newborn was rooming in with me. On about day four, suddenly it occurred to me that the baby needed her diaper changed. It hadn't occurred to me until then because someone else had been changing her diapers, obviously. That may have been a touch of initial maternal indifference. (Downey 1999, 3)

For most mothers with PPD, these feelings lead to anxiety and confusion. They want to feel excited, but they are unable to convince themselves. Unfortunately, many women often translate their guilt and confusion into their maternal role and internalize it as a reflection of their poor parenting skills. Because they do not share in others' joy, they perceive themselves as unfit parents, which only serves to worsen their underlying feelings of worthlessness and inadequacy. The reality, however, is that it is unfair to use their mood as the yardstick for their parental competence.

AGITATION

Interestingly, suicide is less common during postpartum depression than during other times of depression in a woman's life, such as adolescence. Many adolescent women, as well as some older women who may have lost some sense of purpose following retirement or the departure of their children from home, may be more likely to contemplate suicide. In contrast, the mothers of new children may have an internal sense of obligation, responsibility, and purpose that buffers against suicidal thinking and behavior. But where adolescent women may experience suicidality, postpartum women experience agitation. This agitation can assume multiple forms, ranging from poor concentration to restlessness and irritability. Many of those with postpartum depression exhibit anxiety and apprehension about caring for the child, balancing a new lifestyle, and trying to understand and tend to the needs of their child. They also frequently experience insomnia, in this case, having difficulty falling asleep rather than a tendency to wake early in the morning. In fact, they find it hard to get up in the morning, as thoughts of the impending day, maternal responsibilities, or even taking a shower become overwhelming. The comfort of staying in bed is more appealing than the vulnerabilities of being in the outside world or tending to the crying of their infant. Insomnia is made worse for new mothers because their sleep is intermittent and broken by the demands of the child. It is not surprising that they may become easily frustrated with themselves, snap at others, and feel overly anxious, even about bathing the baby.

In fact, some of this agitation may represent a reaction to the underlying feelings of confusion and guilt. Some women may internalize the guilt and say little, but others may become irritable and agitated because they are unable to resolve the confusion about what they feel and how they think they should be responding.

As a case in point, Samanda recently came in to see us for marriage counseling with her husband, Brian. On the fourth session, we went out to the waiting room, but instead of seeing the couple, we saw that Brian was there alone. He mentioned that Samanda had had to stay at home with the children because their babysitter cancelled on them at the last minute. So we spent the session with Brian, and he shared an interesting story about his wife. Following the birth of their second child, she developed significant postpartum depression. She was extremely sad, despondent, lacked energy and initiative, and spent most of the time in bed for three months. At this point, Brian was trying to be as helpful as possible while sustaining full-time employment. He tried to come home early in the evening, care for the children, cook dinner, and clean the house. He reported that it worked well for some time, but one evening, his wife became agitated with him and told him he was not doing enough. He was stunned at first, but his wife later told him that it was because she was feeling inadequate. She lashed out at him in response to her own feelings of irresponsibility. Some of it was a reaction to her own perceived inadequacies and her fear that this meant she did not love her children. At first, Brian was uncertain how to respond, but with our guidance, he was able to understand Samanda's agitation as part of the postpartum process.

SILENCE

Perhaps the most deadly and insidious symptom of postpartum depression is the silence that surrounds these symptoms for many women.

Emily, the woman described at the beginning of this chapter, is a friend of ours. Over dinner one evening, she told us about the difficulty she had had connecting with other mothers of young infants. Immediately after the birth of her child, she wanted to join some groups of like-minded mothers so that she could gain some emotional support and avoid social isolation. But she found neither in the group she attended.

Instead of a group where mothers supported each other and their children's development, she found a lot of isolated mothers who were highly competitive. They made constant and relentless comparisons about their children's motor skills and other developmental milestones, such as when their children raised their heads, how much they weighed, or when they first smiled. Emily had entered the group in hopes of finding community and of being able to talk with others about her postpartum depression, but instead she found more reasons to feel isolated and distant. Many of the other mothers were reluctant to admit to any symptoms of depression, saying instead how easy the delivery was, how well their child slept during the night, and how easily they had lost their "baby fat" with only a little exercise. Emily was eagerly longing for solidarity but found that her symptoms were made worse by feelings of loneliness and greater inadequacy.

The reality is that some of the mothers in this group probably had postpartum depression, but either due to their own fears about their children or their concern for public appearance, they were reticent to discuss their sadness, guilt, and feelings of incompetence. The stigma surrounding PPD remains strong, preventing the emotional support and discussion of treatment options that could help alleviate this common experience.

Postpartum Psychosis

Postpartum psychosis is the third and most rare form of postpartum depression, occurring in one in five hundred births. It is a more severe and serious form of postpartum depression, with rapid onset in the first few days to two weeks after childbirth. The typical course starts with an exaggerated form of the baby blues, with symptoms of insomnia, agitation, and fluctuating mood. Over the next few days, these symptoms give way to more severe symptoms, such as elation, grandiosity, mania, disorganized behavior, and psychosis. Due to the heightened mania in postpartum psychosis, as well as the increased risk for this syndrome among women with bipolar (manic-depressive) disorders, many professionals consider it to be an episode or expression of bipolar disorder (Downey 1999; Payne 2003).

But the hallmark features of this syndrome are delusions and obsessional thoughts regarding the newborn, such as thoughts that the baby is possessed, has special powers, or is destined for a terrible fate. Some women with postpartum psychosis hear disturbing voices telling them to kill the infant. And their ability to assess or gauge the reality of these thoughts and hallucinations is so poor that they may represent a significant danger to themselves and their infants. This is why there is a significant risk of suicide and infanticide among women with postpartum psychosis. No less than 4 percent of women with postpartum psychosis end up killing their child, and 5 percent commit suicide (Ahokas et al. 2001). You may recall the story in the news of Andrea Yates, who was accused of drowning her five children while reportedly in a postpartum psychotic state. The role of postpartum psychosis in contributing to her actions is uncertain, but this shows that postpartum depression and psychosis cannot be treated as trivialities.

Because mothers cannot care for the baby or themselves, postpartum psychosis usually requires inpatient treatment. This may be why psychiatric hospital admissions increase sevenfold for women in the first three months after childbirth compared to the period of prepregnancy (Spinelli 2005). This risk is even higher for first-time mothers (Stocky and Lynch 2000). Again, postpartum psychosis is relatively rare, but the gravity of this condition points to the strong emotional changes that can occur following childbirth. This was true for Yolanda.

HORROR STORY

Yolanda described her second child's birth as though it were a horror story. Yolanda had her first child at age twenty and subsequently suffered from postpartum depression. At the time, she did not seek treatment and eventually worked through most of the symptoms, putting it behind her with the help of her family. Ten years later she had her second child. It did not occur to her that her prior bout of PPD could increase her risk for another episode of depression, particularly because she was in a completely different mind-set.

This time she was not a single mother but had a loving husband and was in a much better social and financial situation to care for her child.

After a very rough pregnancy, Yolanda gave birth to a beautiful eight-pound daughter, Maria. Yolanda quickly realized that while her daughter might be very healthy, a seemingly perfect infant, there was definitely something wrong with Yolanda herself. After the delivery, she felt completely detached from the process. In the hospital, she'd had little interest in her child. Then things got worse. At home she began to think terrible thoughts, like that maybe Maria was a mistake. What was she doing with a new baby—it was hard enough to raise a ten-year-old! Maybe the baby was going to ruin her marriage, sucking her time away from her husband. Then her thoughts turned destructive. She actually thought about suffocating her child and of ways to cover it up, to be relieved of the crying and the constant demand of breastfeeding. Afraid to seek help, Yolanda went on in silent suffering until one day she realized that she had actually ignored Maria's cries and yelps for food and comfort for more than an hour. Yolanda called her mother-in-law, who in turn helped her to seek treatment, including antipsychotic, antidepressant, and antianxiety medication as well as ongoing psychotherapy. After eighteen months of intense treatment, Yolanda finally felt confident as a mother again.

Why Does This Happen?

That the symptoms of PPD happen after delivery suggests that these symptoms of depression are associated with some biological changes occurring in the body of the mother. As with PMS, the fluctuation of estrogen has been implicated as a significant factor contributing to the symptoms of PPD. In short, the development of mood changes and other symptoms of PPD appear to be intimately connected to the rise in estrogen that occurs during pregnancy and its dramatic fall immediately after delivery.

During pregnancy, the placenta begins producing estrogen, adding to the levels of estrogen already generated by the corpus luteum, which you may recall is the solid body that forms when the sack releases a developing egg.

This contribution of added estrogen steadily raises the level to over 100 times the normal amount within the mother's body. Interestingly, symptoms of depression that occur at conception often decrease during the second and third trimesters, which is likely linked to the corresponding change in estrogen levels (Stocky and Lynch 2000). It appears that this change helps to stabilize mood during pregnancy.

With the loss of the placenta at delivery, however, these estrogen levels drop dramatically, typically within twenty-four to forty-eight hours. In over half of all women, the levels of estrogen resemble the levels experienced in menopause and become lower than would be expected if the ovaries had failed (Ahokas et al. 2001). By the fifth postpartum day, the estrogen levels are similar to those prior to pregnancy. Not coincidentally, this is the same day that postpartum blues peak. It is this rise and fall of estrogen, this dramatic change in the hormonal environment, which can persist even into the weeks after childbirth, that may account for some of the depressive symptoms emerging in PPD and postpartum psychosis. The evidence for the role of estrogen in this process can be seen in two types of research: simulation and treatment studies.

Simulation Studies

In simulation studies, the hormonal conditions of pregnancy and postpartum are replicated. In a landmark study, Dr. Miki Bloch and colleagues (2000) from the National Institute of Mental Health re-created the experience of pregnancy and estrogen withdrawal by exposing eight women with and eight women without a history of postpartum depression to high levels of estrogen—matching the levels present during pregnancy—for eight weeks. They then withdrew this estrogen, creating a state similar to the postpartum hormonal environment. What they found was that of the women who had a history of postpartum depression, 63 percent experienced significant depressive symptoms during the postpartum/withdrawal period; of the women without a history of postpartum depression, not one experienced depressive symptoms during the postpartum/withdrawal period. This suggests that estrogen may be directly involved in the development of postpartum depression in a subgroup of women—those with a history of postpartum depression.

Treatment Studies

Treatment studies have assessed whether estrogen replacement therapy (ERT) can significantly reduce the symptoms of postpartum depression. If research shows that replacement of estrogen eliminates or reduces the symptoms of depression, then estrogen levels likely play a part in the emergence of symptoms of postpartum depression. Indeed, most of these studies have shown that the symptoms of depression can be rapidly reduced within the first week of treatment with estrogen supplementation (Dennis 2004; Desai and Jann 2000). And no other factors, such as age, severity and duration of depression episode, concurrent antidepressant medications, or previous psychiatric history influenced the efficacy of estrogen in stabilizing and elevating mood.

This has even been true in the case of postpartum psychosis. In Finland, Dr. Ahokas and his colleagues (2000) discovered that many of the women with postpartum psychosis have abnormally low levels of estrogen, so they administered estrogen in therapeutic doses, which significantly reduced the psychotic symptoms. These therapeutic effects of estrogen administered to women postpartum suggest that the withdrawal or change in estrogen levels may trigger the emergence of depressive symptoms. Estrogen appears to elevate the mood of women postpartum, suggesting that the depleted levels, or more likely the fluctuations, are re-stabilized when estrogen is replaced.

Sequence of Events

This precipitous drop in estrogen level may be the first step in a sequence of biological events that might trigger psychiatric symptoms in the vulnerable woman. Among these biological events are changes in the sensitivities of receptors for neurotransmitters like serotonin and dopamine as well as changes in the levels of other hormones, like thyroid.

SEROTONIN

In particular, the postpartum withdrawal of hormones like estrogen may lead to changes in the serotonin system, including reduced serotonin levels, reduced serotonin uptake, and a depletion of the building blocks that create serotonin. This may account for why SSRIs are increasingly being shown as effective in reversing the symptoms of PPD (Dennis and Stewart 2004; Steiner, Dunn, and Born 2003).

Ironically, it is this evidence for a biochemical neurotransmitter imbalance in postpartum depression that Tom Cruise initially criticized. He fully agreed that there were hormonal changes associated with the postpartum stage, but he denied any science suggesting that emotional and chemical imbalances occur. In doing so, he disregarded the large body of literature suggesting that estrogen is intimately and directly involved in the creation, maintenance, and breakdown of serotonin levels, which have themselves been directly connected with depression. By criticizing the use of Paxil, and by saying "there's no such thing as a chemical imbalance," he effectively turned a blind eye to the evidence suggesting that the drastic withdrawal of estrogen following delivery would invariably have an effect on the sensitivity of receptors involved with serotonin.

THYROID

In addition, one of the by-products of the exodus of estrogen and these reduced serotonin levels appears to be abnormal thyroid functioning. The thyroid is a gland that regulates the rate of metabolism in the body. The underactivity of this gland, which results in a lower metabolism or rate of energy, has been associated with depressive symptoms, in particular, sadness, reduced energy and initiative, weight gain, and despondency. During pregnancy, the thyroid enlarges and a state of *hyperthyroidism* follows, which provides more energy for and elevated mood in the mother. However, a state of *hypothyroidism* occurs in 7 percent of women during the six months following delivery, which has been associated with reduced motivation and energy, as well as greater sadness and weight gain. There is even some evidence suggesting that up to 12 percent of postpartum women have antibodies against the thyroid hormones (Hendrick, Altshuler, and Suri 1998), creating a state of hypothyroidism that increases a woman's vulnerability to depression.

Sensitivity, Not Absolute Levels

Despite the strong evidence for the role of estrogen in depression, it is important to note that these symptoms are not due to differences in the overall levels of hormones. The dramatic drop in estrogen following delivery occurs in all women, so it is inaccurate to say that depression in PPD is simply due to the withdrawal of estrogen. If that were the case, all women would develop PPD. Therefore, PPD is not a dysfunction of estrogen change alone but rather reflects a women's differential sensitivity to these changes. The normal rise and fall in estrogen that occurs during pregnancy and after may render some women more vulnerable to depression. In short, these estrogen changes, primarily for a certain subset of women, may prompt a cascade of changes in serotonin, thyroid function, and other systems that result in depression.

Conclusion

Postpartum depression represents one more developmental point in a woman's life when her mood may be altered by estrogen changes. Because this form of depression is prevalent, its legitimacy as a condition is seldom in question. In fact, most medical professionals agree that postpartum blues and depression may be a natural artifact of the delivery process. But what may be underappreciated, however, is the level of the impact this condition can have on a woman's life. The length of time that it may persist can have significant implications for the emotional state and functioning of the mother and the quality of her attachment with her child. Women with emotional indifference or sadness may not be able to bond with the same quality of secure attachment as those without PPD. This makes it critical for women to embrace these symptoms despite the stigma. It also makes it extremely important for medical professionals to respond to women's concerns about postpartum depression without simply chalking it up to a natural by-product of childbirth.

CHAPTER 5

The Three Stages of Menopause

Sometimes she breezes in with a smile on her face and greets everyone in the office. Other days she stomps in and snaps at the first person she sees. A quick glance at her and you might think, "Why does she look so sad today when she seemed fine yesterday?" Not only is her mood unpredictable, but so is the temperature of her office. During the morning, she cranks up the heat to take the chill off, but later she turns the temperature so low you think you are in the Arctic. There seems to be no rhyme or reason to these fluctuations: they occur in the winter and the summer, the morning and the afternoon. What is going on? Welcome to perimenopause. The hot flashes, the unpredictable bursts of irritability, and the sadness are common symptoms of this life phase that previous generations have called "the change."

Although we will concentrate on the connection between mood and declining estrogen levels during menopause in this chapter, it is important to keep in mind that mood can also be related to other symptoms of menopause. In fact, the symptoms of menopause such as poor sleep, night sweats, and weight gain can have a direct impact on mood (expressed as irritability, anxiety, and depression, for example), not to mention loss of interest in sex and possible memory loss. In this chapter we will explore the stages of menopause, the multiple symptoms associated with menopause, and the link between estrogen and depression. Let's begin with the stages of menopause.

Stages of Menopause

Perimenopause, menopause, and postmenopause can be thought of as the three stages of the menopause transition. It is during these stages that ovarian hormone production begins to fluctuate and eventually decline, resulting in significant biological, clinical, and endocrinal changes (WHO 1981).

Perimenopause

Have you ever heard a woman, perhaps your grandmother or mother, use the term "the change"? Most likely they were referring to *perimenopause* or the stage when your hormone levels noticeably change and your menstrual cycle becomes irregular. In as early as her midthirties, a woman may begin to experience the initial symptoms of perimenopause, but most women will not experience any recognizable perimenopausal symptoms until they are well into their forties. In fact, most women begin the transition in their midforties and usually take four to five years to complete it (Woods and Mitchell 2004), although some women will not make the transition until they are in their fifties. This onset is typically associated with irregular periods, beginning with the shortening of menstrual cycles, coupled with an increased flow and midcycle spotting, and ending with fewer but longer cycles (a process called *skipping*) (Mitchell, Woods, and Mariella 2000). We will discuss these cycle changes later in the chapter.

Menopause

In *menopause*, your menstrual cycle is no longer changing; instead, it ceases to exist. This event brings mixed feelings for many women. The absence of a period means relief for some, but it also means the loss of the ability to have children. The medical term "menopause" refers to the permanent ending of menstruation in a woman due to the decreased production of estrogen and progesterone by the ovaries. It is defined as the time when there have been no menstrual periods for twelve consecutive months, and it marks the end of fertility. The mean age of menopause is typically fifty-one, but some (for example, smokers) can have their final period one to two years earlier.

Postmenopause

In some ways menopause is not a life phase, but a threshold. Once you cross over the twelve-month mark, your menopause moment is over. You are now *postmenopausal*.

Perimenopausal Transition

Now that we've given a quick overview of each stage of menopause, let's spend more time discussing the transition between perimenopause and menopause. Most women are not going to run out and get their hormone levels tested every few weeks or months, so bleeding patterns have typically been used to determine the three stages of menopausal transition (Mitchell, Woods, and Mariella 2000).

1. **Early stage:** Flow and/or cycle length changes.

2. **Middle stage:** Cycle is irregular without skipping.

3. **Late stage:** Menstrual cycles are skipped.

This is just a guideline. Every woman's experience is different. Approximately 75 percent of all women do report changes in their cycle. Typically the cycle becomes less regular, sometimes lighter in flow and/or shorter in length. But some women experience heavier bleeding for an even longer period—sometimes even ten days at a time. They may also have spotting between periods. In 79 percent of women, the initial change is in flow or regularity, occurring before any skipping of the period (Mitchell, Woods, and Mariella 2000). You should discuss each observed pattern with your doctor.

Can these stages actually correlate to changes in mood? Possibly, although there is very little research to connect the exact menopause stage to a distinct profile of mood symptoms. Researchers are busy trying to measure hormone levels and determine if in fact there is a distinct profile of mood and cognitive changes related to certain levels of declining estrogen (Eriksson et al. 2006). While we may not have determined the exact profile for mood and menopause stages, we can certainly examine what it looks like in real women.

Jennifer's Story

Jennifer is forty-four and a single mother. She works as a social worker in a community-based mental health center in California. She was recently promoted to director of training, which is an exciting challenge, but it also means that she is working even longer hours than she used to. This is hard for Jennifer because she is already feeling a little stressed out and blue about life. On top of a stressful job, Jennifer is trying to raise her fourteen-year-old daughter without any help. She loves her daughter dearly, and she is struggling to create stability in their home life. This is a real challenge because Jennifer feels as if her internal world is a train wreck waiting to happen. On this train trip called life she is on the fast track, in motion, but feels as if she will veer off course at any moment.

And the worst part is that initially she could not figure out why she felt down, out of sorts, and frequently irritable. As Jennifer tried to piece together her mood issues, she noticed several physical symptoms, such as weight gain and insomnia. Around this time she also realized that her period was irregular. She hadn't skipped any periods, but she couldn't predict when she would get her next period. Sometimes it would come on time, yet other times it would come forty to fifty days after the previous one. On top of that, a few years before, the nature of her period had changed, with a heavier flow but lasting fewer days. After discussing her life story with us at the seminar, it was determined that Jennifer was in the middle stage of perimenopause. After learning more about perimenopause, this made sense to Jennifer, as she has many of the menopause symptoms and her mood was very unpredictable. With the social stressors of work, raising her daughter, and being alone, Jennifer realized she needed more information and help; she needed to know more about perimenopause and how it might be impacting her ability to cope with her current level of stress.

Onset & Duration

As we reflect on Jennifer's story, we begin to realize that her mood changes are most likely related to the onset of perimenopause, which probably started a few years ago, when she was forty or forty-one. The typical age of onset is forty to forty-four, but perimenopause can begin anywhere from age thirty-five to fifty-five, with the median age of inception at forty-seven to forty-eight years old (Hardy and Kuh 1999). Perimenopause is thought to be a three- to four-year period just prior to menopause, but many clinicians maintain that perimenopause can last for as long as five to fifteen years. Whether it is a few years or longer, many women are likely to notice at least a few, if not several, of the symptoms associated with this phase of hormonal change. Of these symptoms, depression can be among the most troubling and one that can persist into menopause and postmenopause.

Menopause & Postmenopause Transition

At first, it is almost impossible to know when a woman is going from perimenopause to menopause. Because perimenopause is defined as irregular periods, including skipping, a woman might not realize that she is in the final menopause transition for several months. The symptoms of perimenopause and menopause are similar, and the transition can be hard to pinpoint until the woman has skipped enough periods that she realizes, in hindsight, that she's probably seen the last one. If this pattern continues for twelve consecutive months, with no menstrual cycle, then the woman has officially become postmenopausal. The symptoms of this natural menopause transition are similar to those experienced in perimenopause due to further declines in estrogen.

For some women, there is no twelve-month transition to menopause. Instead, there is a dramatic ushering in of the postmenopausal phase because of surgery. Let's take a look at the natural versus surgical avenues to menopause, because each can have a significantly different impact on mood and therefore may call for a different approach in treatment.

Two Types of Menopause

There are women who make the transition to menopause on their own. They may or may not experience significant perimenopause symptoms as their estrogen levels decline, but they eventually stop having a menstrual cycle. During this transition, these women may or may not seek help, depending upon the impact of their symptoms on their life as well as their overall attitude about menopause. This transition seems subtle, although it may not be for the individual woman as she suffers through physical and emotional symptoms, which can persist for years.

Whether this journey is difficult or easy, it is certainly a sharp contrast to the second avenue of menopause—surgery. When a woman has a hysterectomy, her uterus and possibly her ovaries are removed. Women have hysterectomies for a variety of reasons, including fibroids, endometriosis, prolapse of the vagina, pelvic adhesions (scarring), uncontrollable or heavy bleeding and pelvic pain, precancerous cells, or cancer of the cervix, uterus, or ovaries. Women who have a hysterectomy abruptly enter menopause, resulting in a condition called *surgical menopause*. To find out what this looks like in real women, let's meet Joan and Jean.

Joan was finally a grandmother, an event she had been anticipating for years, and yet she felt utterly depressed. There seemed to be no good reason for her sadness. She had recently retired and finally had time to go golfing with her husband. She was looking forward to traveling a bit more, going on some trips to see her daughter and new grandbaby, and planning a cruise around the world. Socially things seemed in place, but physically there was a laundry list of complaints. Being postmenopausal was not easy. Joan had a few new aches and pains; then there were the dry skin and creaky bones. But most challenging was the blues. These feelings of depression snuck up on her, without any real direct link to her life's situation. Was this sadness linked to a hidden cause within menopause, such as low levels of estrogen?

Unlike her older sister Joan, Jean knew why she was depressed. She was also pretty certain that it was connected in some way to estrogen. Three months before, Jean had to have an emergency hysterectomy. First there was the constant bleeding, and then there was the scare that maybe she had cancer of the uterus. Her doctor recommended the removal of both her uterus and ovaries. Now a few months after the surgery, she was physically recovering well, but her mood was bordering on full-blown depression. She felt no comfort from her family or friends. The world seemed bleak. She had declined her doctor's suggestion to take estrogen replacement therapy, but now she was thinking twice about her decision.

These two stories are real-life examples of how dramatically different the journey of menopause can be, although the impact can be severe no matter which avenue you take. Now that we have defined the stages as well as the natural and surgical types of menopause, we can begin to examine the symptoms of menopause and how they might relate to the connection between estrogen and depression.

Symptoms of Menopause

Are you or a loved one currently in the early stages of menopause? Perhaps you are in the postmenopausal state. Whether you are in perimenopause, menopause, or postmenopause, your symptoms may look like the ones we have listed below. The symptoms of menopause, both physical and mood states, are a direct result of declining levels of estrogen. You may want to use this as a checklist of sorts, placing a check next to any symptom you are experiencing.

- Irregular periods
- Fatigue
- Hot flashes
- Anxiety
- Night sweats
- Irritability
- Disturbed sleep
- Depression

- Vaginal dryness
- Low sex drive
- Headaches
- Infertility
- Sore breasts
- Frustration
- Weight gain
- Poor memory

- Constipation
- Inattention
- Wrinkling
- Muscle and joint pain
- Loss of bone density
- Heart disease
- Bloating

If you only checked a few items, there are numerous possible explanations for what is going on with your body, mind, or mood. But if you checked several of these symptoms, say, at least five or more, there is a greater likelihood that you are experiencing some stage of menopause, particularly if you are over forty and have experienced changes in your menstrual cycle. No matter your age or the number of symptoms you checked, you may want to consult a doctor about your health profile, including your mood.

Symptoms of menopause are complex. Specifically, declining levels of estrogen produce the physical changes mentioned above and estrogen deficiency also results in mood changes, thus the focus of this book. But to complicate matters further, some changes in mood may be a result of the physical changes rather than the estrogen deficiency, per se. Given the risk of experiencing depression during menopause, it is important to discuss both mood and physical changes that occur with menopause as a result of estrogen deficiency. It is also important to discuss the complex interaction of estrogen, mood, and these physical changes.

The Blues: Depression & Menopause

For about two hundred years, the stages of the menopause transition have been associated with depression. Despite this observed link, there has not always been clear evidence as to whether women in the menopause transition are more at risk for depression. At present, the rates of depression in perimenopausal women appear to be significant. Dr. Novaes and colleagues (1998) reported that almost 50 percent of perimenopausal women have had some type of psychiatric symptoms, with almost one-third diagnosed with a depressive disorder. Drs. Halbreich and Kahn (2001) also noted a strong relationship between perimenopause and mood symptoms. Our own review of the literature indicated that 22 to 50 percent of women in perimenopause experience depression (Miller and Rogers 2005). Finally, Dr. Cohen and colleagues (2005) recently reviewed numerous large studies and asserted that there is a strong association between the risk of depression and menopause. After making the transition to the postmenopausal state, we know that approximately 10 to 20 percent of these women meet criteria for a formal diagnosis of major depression. In other words, one or two of every ten postmenopausal women have significant depression that somehow affects their ability to function optimally in everyday life. For example, they may miss work or cannot be as productive as they would like to be at work or in the home; they may avoid social situations with family or friends or have less interest in their hobbies or personal hygiene.

Because we focus on depression and menopause in this chapter, it is important to keep in mind the definition of major depression that most medical doctors, psychologists, other therapists, and researchers use to define the significance or seriousness of mood disturbance. From previous chapters, you may recall the following formal diagnosis from the *Diagnostic and Statistical Manual of Mental Disorders* (DSM-IV) (APA 1994). The criteria to meet for major depression are as follows:

- A woman must report five or more of the following depressive symptoms:
  - Depressed mood most of the day
  - Diminished interest in usual activities
  - Psychomotor agitation or retardation
  - Insomnia or *hypersomnia* (excessive sleep) daily
  - Change in weight or appetite
  - Recurrent thoughts of death
  - Feelings of worthlessness or guilt
  - Diminished concentration
- The symptoms must be present for a two-week period and represent a change from previous functioning.
- The symptoms must interfere with work or school or usual social activities and relationships.
- The symptoms are not due to substance abuse or a medical condition.

As we have seen throughout this book, estrogen levels are often linked to depression. In postmenopausal women, it is the estrogen deficiency that may increase the risk of major depression (Palinkas and Barrett-Conner 1992). This increased risk appears to be greatest in the first two years of menopause, when the body must adjust to a dramatic decline of estrogen—a drop of approximately 80 percent, according to van der Schouw and Grobbee (2005).

This is not to say that postmenopausal women will not have depression after two years, but the risk is greatest at the beginning.

Beyond the Definition & Numbers

Researchers typically agree that at least 10 percent of menopausal women have a formal diagnosis of depression, and 50 percent report some symptoms such as anxiety, irritability, depression, and mood swings. Many women feel they have no control over these mood issues. Other women have only minimal mood effects during the menopause transition. Building on our discussion of how estrogen influences the brain, particularly the biochemistry related to mood functioning, we will now discuss why women are more at risk for these estrogen-related mood issues during menopause.

Dr. Rasgon and colleagues (2005) from Stanford published a review regarding perimenopausal mental disorders. They are careful to point out that not all researchers confirm the existence of depression during perimenopause, but they also offer insight into the reigning theories of why women may become more depressed during the menopause transition:

- Neurobiological theory: Declining estrogen is the cause of depression.

- Domino theory: Depression is secondary to the vasomotor (physical) changes.

- Psychosocial theory: Depression is a result of changing relationships and demands in a woman's life.

Neurobiological Theory & Estradiol Levels

In chapter 1, we discussed at length how estrogen influences the biochemistry of the brain and its ability to regulate mood. This is the neurobiological theory. You may recall that estrogen occurs in three natural forms. One of these is estradiol. Doctors are able to measure estradiol and note that its levels drop significantly one to two years before menopause and continue to drop during the first few years of the postmenopause phase (Woods and

Mitchell 2004). Dr. Freeman and colleagues (2004) found that fluctuations in estradiol levels were significantly associated with symptoms of depression, hot flashes (sometimes called *flushes*), and poor sleep. This suggests that the decline in estrogen levels associated with perimenopause may have a direct effect on the emergence of depression during this period. Dr. Rasgon and colleagues (2005) from Stanford also believe that the successful treatment of depression with hormone replacement therapy (HRT) suggests support for both the neurobiological and the domino theory as causes for depression.

Domino Theory

The *domino theory* is sometimes called the *symptom hypothesis*. This theory proposes that women are more at risk for depression secondary to their experience of menopausal symptoms, that is, women become depressed in response to their other menopausal symptoms, which were a result of declines in estrogen levels. One change leads to the next change, resulting in a domino effect. Estrogen has a significant effect on multiple parts of a woman's body, so the decline of estrogen will impact each aspect of the woman's body.

VASOMOTOR SYMPTOMS

When trying to understand the domino theory, it is critical to become familiar with the term "vasomotor symptoms," which will pop up time after time when reading any type of scientific literature on perimenopause. The term "vasomotor" relates to the system of nerves connected to the blood vessels. When this term is used to describe symptoms of the menopausal woman, it usually refers to the changes in the nerve–blood vessel connection that bring about physical symptoms, such as hot flashes, headaches, and night sweats. Let's take a closer look at some of the specific vasomotor symptoms, which are important because they impact sleep, and in turn, mood and emotional functioning.

Hot flashes. Sometimes called *hot flashes* or *flushes*, these "surges" of heat often cause significant discomfort in women. Blood vessels dilate and bring large amounts of blood to the surface of the skin. There is an actual rise in the body temperature of up to 7 degrees. This is typically accompanied by perspiration and increased heart rate. A hot flash usually lasts for three to five minutes, but it may become so bad that the person faints. The hot flash may also bring a sense of dread or anxiety for the moment (Huston, Sleath, and Rubin 2001). Approximately 75 percent of women experience hot flashes. About 10 to 15 percent report that hot flashes are debilitating (Kronenberg, Mallory, and Downey 1993). Women may experience one to four a day or night, and this symptom is likely to peak in the final year of perimenopause or before the final menses (Avis et al. 1993). They continue into menopause, with 80 percent of women reporting that they have hot flashes for at least two more years. But others report that hot flashes persist for somewhere between five to ten years.

Remember the case of Jennifer, presented earlier in the chapter? She described her hot flashes as almost disabling at times. She would feel so hot that she could not concentrate and had to take off her suit jacket, crank up the air-conditioning, and try to calm down. After speaking with her, we realized that her situation is consistent with the domino theory. She reported that her hot flashes significantly disrupted her daily life, leaving her feeling depressed over the inability to control her own body and mood.

Headaches. Many women report an increase in headaches, including migraines, during perimenopause. Dr. Wang and colleagues (2003) offer insight into this relationship. They note a link between migraine headaches and hormones. For those who already suffer from migraines, there is an increase of attacks for 26 to 60 percent of these women during the menopause transition. Finally, a history of PMS or surgical menopause (removal of ovaries) also increases the frequency of migraines.

If you think about it, it makes sense that headaches might contribute to the domino effect of depression. Many women who report a significant history of headaches also feel disabled and depressed in some way. They miss more work, social events, and opportunities to spend time as they would like. As headache duration or frequency increases, so do feelings of frustration and ineffectiveness, putting women at greater risk for sadness.

Night sweats. This is a feeling of warmth, possibly a flush, which spreads over the body and can include perspiration. Some clinicians describe it as an actual fever, lasting a few minutes, with heart rate and body temperature rising, followed by a chill. It is difficult to know the extent to which this occurs but consider that there is actually a whole pajama line advertised on the Internet for women who are experiencing night sweats. That tells us that it is a bothersome symptom—one that can interfere with a woman's overall well-being.

Sleep disturbances. Women typically begin to have trouble sleeping during the late stage of perimenopause, with continued difficulties into the postmenopause phase. Low levels of progesterone (a hormone related to estrogen) have been linked with a longer period between stage one and REM sleep, resulting in less time spent in deep restful sleep. Less restful sleep and night sweats result in an overall feeling of fatigue in the morning. It is difficult to experience interrupted sleep, night after night. Some of you may have had that experience when you had a new baby. After a few weeks, let alone a few months, you feel like a zombie. A menopausal woman may experience that zombie-like effect, if the sleep disturbance is significant. One of the domino effects of feeling like a zombie is that you are more easily moved to tears and that you are more sensitive about things. The fatigue itself can lead to feelings of depression. As these sleep disturbances suggest, it is key that we understand how body and mind are linked, including the impact of one's health on mood functioning.

HEALTH CHANGES

It is important to understand these potentially debilitating vasomotor symptoms. It is also critical to understand the health changes that come along with perimenopause as well as their potential impact on mood.

Osteoporosis. Probably the most publicized health change in perimenopause is *osteoporosis*. Sometimes called the *brittle bone disease*, this is a loss of bone mineral density. Estrogen facilitates the uptake of calcium and activates the cells responsible for bone remodeling. Essentially, estrogen and calcium maintain the "scaffolding" of bones in our bodies. Declines in estrogen can lead to bone disintegration and loss of bone mass. This loss can be substantial—as much as 50 percent of bone loss in the spine and 30 percent of loss in other bones within twenty years of menopause. Most bone loss occurs in the spine, wrists, collarbone, and hips. This condition is very painful, crippling, and even life threatening. However, it has no early warning signs, so many women are unaware of it.

Is this really related in some way to mood functioning? You bet. Consider, for example, Marlene, a new grandmother. She was thrilled to have a first grandchild and planned to be the primary caregiver when her daughter returned to work as a neuropsychologist. However, these dreams were quickly shattered. Because of her advancing age and brittle bones, when she took a very mild spill, she ended up with compound fractures in her ankle. It was several months before she was mobile and able to care even for herself, let alone for her new grandbaby. The physical recovery was difficult but so was the mental recovery. She suffered a significant bout of depression, directly related to this medical situation. Declining health has a direct impact on mood.

Muscles and joints. Not only bones are impacted; muscle begins to lose bulk, strength, and coordination. Joints can become stiff, particularly with exercise, and they can also swell, resulting in less mobility. These symptoms are typically related to a decrease in collagen and a higher rate of osteoporosis, and can impact women very early in the menopause transition.

Take Ellen for example. She was an avid runner, often tackling two or three marathons a year. As perimenopause began to take hold, she felt more achy and stiff. Even with supplements, she reported that she could run only two to three times a week, rather than the four to six times a week she used to run. Did this have an impact on her mood? She would definitely say yes because running had been her main method to release stress, but she could no longer engage in it daily.

Stomach and bowels. Due to declining levels of estrogen, constipation can be a common problem in menopause. Estrogen is known to facilitate bowel movements, while progesterone hinders them, resulting in dry, pebble-like stools. Also, as people age, small pockets of tissue can balloon from the bowel, resulting in a condition called *diverticula*. Food can get trapped in these pockets, become stale, and produce gas, which in turn distends the abdomen. Slower bowels, distended abdomens, and bloating can be common in menopause. It is hard to say that something as uncomfortable as constipation can cause depression, but it can impact mood for the woman who already has a long list of other physical changes.

Cholesterol and cardiovascular problems. Did you know that heart disease is the number one cause of death for women over fifty? In fact, women are twelve times more likely to die from a heart attack than from breast cancer. Younger women are at less risk for heart disease than men, thanks to estrogen, which increases *high density lipoprotein* (HDL), which is the good cholesterol that helps to prevent the narrowing of the artery walls. Also remember that we described estrogen as the "exterminator" in chapter 1; because estrogen is able to inhibit or clear out toxic free radicals in the blood vessels, premenopausal women may be at lower risk for heart attacks and strokes than same-age men. This protection changes with menopause. *Low density cholesterol* (LDL), sometimes called "bad cholesterol" or "bad lipids," rises rapidly in menopausal women, doubling the risk of coronary heart disease after menopause compared to the risk for men of the same age. While LDL carries cholesterol for cell-building needs, it also leaves behind excess cholesterol on artery walls and in tissues, thus an excess of LDL can increase the risk for heart disease. It is not only declining estrogen that increases the risk of heart disease, but also obesity, high blood pressure, diabetes, smoking, high cholesterol, and lack of exercise. As the domino theory suggests, each of these physical factors can contribute to depressive symptoms as women experience uncontrollable changes in their body. Turning in another direction, the psychosocial theory addresses depression that can result from changing relationships and demands in a woman's life. Unlike the other two theories, there is no direct link between estrogen and depression within the psychosocial theory, yet it is important to explore.

Psychosocial Theory

We all know that when we are stressed, we are more likely to feel depressed. Researchers Drs. Woods and Mitchell from the University of Washington in Seattle report that at least seven major studies, including their own Seattle Midlife Women's Health Study, have found stress to be the dominant factor related to depressed mood in women during midlife years. Specifically, health problems and difficulties in relationships contributed to stress (Woods and Mitchell 1997). Others have indicated that caring for aging parents and adolescents, financial worries, divorce, death of loved ones, and changes in career contribute to midlife stress. You might argue that both men and women experience an increase of stress in midlife. But from a social standpoint, we know that an increase in responsibilities is more likely to fall on the shoulders of women; they are more likely to be the caregivers for children and aging parents. We also know that women are more likely than men to become depressed when faced with the adversity of stress. Women are three times as likely as men to become depressed in response to a stressful event (Woods and Mitchell 1997). This may be connected to the idea that women are more likely to engage in *ruminative thinking*, which is the repetitive focus on distress, causes, and consequences. A woman's psychosocial situation is often impacted by her personal experience.

THE MIND-BODY CONNECTION

Experiencing stress is one psychosocial factor. There are several other symptoms in the menopausal transition that may also have psychosocial impact or mediate the emergence of depression during this life phase. For example, breast soreness, vaginal dryness, weight gain, collagen deficiency, and declining sex drive are physical symptoms that can also have significant psychosocial impact on a woman's mood and her relationships. Let's take a closer look at these additional symptoms.

Breast soreness. Some women experience sore breasts during PMS. This is typically associated with fluid retention in the breast tissue. This discomfort is called *mastalgia* and can become extremely painful. It typically occurs after the age of forty or the onset of perimenopause, and it can occur at any time in the month. Note that saturated fatty oils can aggravate the problem. While mastalgia is benign, discomfort like this should be discussed with a doctor to rule out breast cancer. While definitely uncomfortable, breast soreness is likely to improve with time.

Vaginal dryness. During the late stage of perimenopause, women often report vaginal dryness. This symptom seems to increase during the very end of perimenopause and for the first few years of postmenopause. Along with vaginal dryness, there may be discomfort in urinating, an urgent and frequent desire to urinate, or dribbling due to weak sphincter muscles. These symptoms are something many women avoid talking about, whether it is to their doctor, friends, or sexual partner. In fact, only four out of ten women consult their doctor for these symptoms. This avoidance can result in silent suffering. While certainly a very personal symptom, it is an important one to mention when talking to health care professionals. Relief is available, typically with topical lubricants and cream. It is also important to discuss this symptom with your sexual partner as it may be linked to a change in desire for sex or the pleasure associated with it.

Weight gain. As menopause approaches, estrogen levels decline, and metabolic rates decrease. Some researchers have indicated that the average woman gains about five pounds during the transition to menopause, but 20 percent of women may gain ten pounds or more during this time (Woods and Mitchell 2004; Wing et al. 1991). Dr. Wing and colleagues (1991, 1992) found that weight gain was often associated with rising blood insulin levels and that these levels were highest in women with more abdominal fat and higher *body mass index* (BMI), which is a way to gauge total body fat using a person's weight and height. It is important to remember that diet, exercise, and alcohol consumption can contribute to fluctuations in weight. There is presently a hot debate on how weight impacts your longevity. At first it was thought that those who are within normal weight limits (BMI of 18.5 to 25) and those who are "overweight" (BMI of 25 to 30) live longer than those who are underweight (BMI of less than 18.5) or those who are considered obese (BMI of over 30) (Flegal et al. 2005). However, additional research has now clarified that even being "overweight" during midlife (fifty years old) increases the risk of death by 20 to 40 percent and that those who are obese are two to three times more likely to die within ten years (Adams et al. 2006). Using this guideline, gaining a few pounds during menopause might not impact your overall health unless you are already overweight; however, if you are overweight or obese you will want to think about working with your doctor and improving your lifestyle choices to decrease your weight and mortality risk.

Collagen deficiency. "Wrinkled like a prune" is a colorful description that refers to the loss of collagen that occurs naturally with aging but that is particularly noticeable with declining estrogen levels. While some collagen loss may not occur until much later in life, the advent of perimenopause and collagen deficiency can result in numerous symptoms. The skin becomes dry, wrinkled, and flaky. It is more likely to bruise, wounds heal more slowly, veins are prominent, and patches of brown pigmentation may occur. Nails are more brittle. Hair may become dull, dry, and thin; hair loss and split ends are more likely to occur. Eyes are dry, perhaps with dark circles; lumps of yellow fat may appear on the whites of the eyes; night vision declines; and red blood vessels are more evident, giving the appearance of "bloodshot eyes." Gums recede and bleed; periodontal disease causes bad breath. The mouth may crack at the corners, and the tongue becomes scalloped, thinner, and smoother. The loss of collagen can have a significant impact on your overall personal appearance, which in turn can impact self-esteem and even mood.

Decreased sex drive. Given that menopausal women may have hot flashes, vaginal dryness, sore breasts, weight gain, aching muscles, and moodiness, it's no wonder so many women are saying, "Not tonight honey." Yes, a decline in sex drive can occur in the menopausal transition. People don't agree as to how many women experience a lower sex drive. Most researchers and menopause information sites report that 20 to 45 percent of women have a lower sex drive during menopause. This can have a significant impact on body image, self-esteem, mood, and relationships. Remember Jennifer? In addition to dealing with life stresses and perimenopausal physical symptoms, Jennifer also felt pressure from her parents to find a husband, yet she struggled with issues of body image and insecurity. She felt that she had to battle her own internal process before she was ready to embrace the dating world and possibly a new relationship. Low sex drive is just one symptom that can be a result of peri-menopause, but as with all symptoms, each woman's experience will vary and much will depend on her personal perception.

Impact of symptoms. Is there really a connection between the symptoms described above and a woman's mood? That all depends upon the woman. For many, the answer is yes. As most of us can imagine, one of these symptoms, let alone several of them working together, can significantly impact a woman's perception of her body and of herself as a sexual being. This can have a direct impact on her self-esteem, her desire to relate to her sexual partner, or even the view of herself within a social context. This is not to say that all women are impacted by these symptoms or feel as if their relationships or social status suffer because of physical changes related to menopause, but many women do report a connection. When physical changes impact a relationship, there is an increase of stress in that *dyad* (the couple's system of relating to each other). As we learned earlier, stress is often the number one contributor to depression in women. As clinicians and as friends we must carefully consider the interplay between the physical symptoms of menopause and their impact on relationships, social functioning, and mood.

Personal Perceptions

It is important to remember that each woman perceives these symptoms differently, in terms of the pain or discomfort associated with them as well as the significance or importance of the symptoms within her own life context. There are many common myths about menopause, like the ones in table 5.1. Depending upon a woman's perception, these myths may feel like reality to her.

TABLE 5.1: COMMON MYTHS ABOUT MENOPAUSE

It only happens when you are old.
Menopausal women lose their looks.
Depression in menopause is just a state of mind.
Memory loss is inevitable.
Menopausal women are no longer interested in sex.
Calcium is the best treatment for symptoms.
All treatments can cause breast cancer.

To best understand these personal perceptions and possible myths, let's return to Jennifer. The irregularity of her period and the accompanying hot flashes and irritability may be very disturbing to her, particularly within the context of her already stressful life (director of training, high caseload of clients, single parent raising a teenage daughter). On a scale of 1 to 10, she may rate her discomfort and the impact on her ability to function in her normal life as a 7, which means she feels very affected by these symptoms. Jennifer's sister, Lisa (the woman in chapter 3 with PMS), might describe her symptoms as a 10, or extremely disabling, in that she is not able to work during the weeks that she is experiencing these symptoms. When someone is experiencing their symptoms at a 10, or even a 7, this is likely to have a significant impact on their mood, potentially resulting in more depression.

Jennifer and Lisa's assessments of their symptoms may be very different from how other women may view their symptoms. For example, recently we were training a young male graduate student on the art of the clinical interview. This is the first step taken before conducting a lengthy memory evaluation. Part of the clinical interview involves asking women questions about their reproductive history, current functioning, and mood. Symptoms are typically rated as *none*, *mild*, *moderate*, or *severe* on these interview questionnaires. This student asked the patient, Margaret, if she was experiencing any *loss of libido* (decline in her sex drive). She casually answered, "Yes, for quite some time." He then responded, "Well, would you rate this as severe, then?" She looked at him with shock and responded "No!" She added, "It doesn't really bother me, so I would say none or mild." At that moment, this future psychologist realized his mistake. To a twenty-five-year-old man, a significant loss of libido seems like a severe symptom, yet this particular menopausal woman was not bothered by it.

Each person's perception is unique. Some menopausal women will not be bothered by loss of libido or other symptoms, while others will be. Margaret's perception of her menopausal symptoms is a contrast to the experiences of Lisa and Jennifer. Why is Margaret's perception so different? Perhaps she is not as biochemically affected by the declines in estrogen as Lisa and Jennifer. Perhaps she has no history of depression symptoms, has a more relaxed lifestyle, and feels more support within her family or social network. These three women could potentially experience menopause symptoms of the same intensity, but their perception, attitudes, and past history affect how much the symptoms impact their mood and daily functioning. Thus, personal history and individual perception are keys to better understanding how symptoms affect each person and to what degree they are bothersome, or worse.

Tangled Cluster

The cause of depression in menopause is possibly a tangled cluster of the theories just described rather than simply one direct link. In sum, biological, psychological, and social factors are most likely all contributing to the complex interaction of estrogen and mood. From earlier chapters, we know that women are more prone to depression given a fluctuation in estrogen. We know that vasomotor and other symptoms are present during the menopause transition. Certainly physical changes can cause mood changes. Increases in life's demands can be taxing. If you take all three theories into account, we can perhaps arrive at a comprehensive conclusion—women are at risk for depression during the menopause transition. Reality seems to bear this out: women within menopause are three times more likely to be depressed than are their younger, nonmenopausal cohort (Freeman et al. 2004). Dr. Freeman and colleagues (2006) also discovered that even women without a history of depression were at risk for depression during the menopause transition.

Additional Risk Factors for Depression

Are all women at risk for depression during the menopause transition? Given that estrogen is declining in menopause, we could say yes, based on what we have learned thus far about the connection between estrogen and mood. However, some women in menopause might be at an increased risk for depression, so let's explore the additional risk factors for depression during this period.

Previous History of Depression & Anxiety

Dr. Hay and colleagues (1994) reported that at least 35 percent of women with a past or current depressive episode were likely to experience another episode during perimenopause. Women between the ages of forty-five and fifty-four are most at risk for recurrent depression. Usually the depression occurs within four years of the final menstrual cycle.

Just recently, Dr. Freeman and colleagues (2005) reported that anxious women tend to have the most severe and frequent vasomotor symptoms. Which comes first? In their study, baseline anxiety predicted the occurrence of hot flashes eight to twelve months later. What this means is that women who were already anxious experienced more severe vasomotor symptoms as the length of perimenopause increased.

Premenstrual Syndrome

Remember that we discussed PMS at length in chapter 3, including the link between fluctuating estrogen levels and the impact on mood. Recent research has asserted that women with premenstrual syndrome (PMS) are at greater risk for menopausal symptoms, such as decreased libido, poor sleep, hot flashes, and depressed mood (Freeman et al. 2004), than women who have not had PMS. In fact, the women in their study were twice as likely to report hot flashes and depressed mood if they had had a history of PMS.

Length of Perimenopause

In the early 1990s, Drs. Avis and McKinlay conducted the Massachusetts Women's Health Study. They found that a longer perimenopause transition correlated with an increased risk for depression. Prolonged perimenopause can be defined as more than two years (Avis et al. 1994).

This makes sense if we stop to think about it. If you enter a phase where your estrogen levels are fluctuating, the longer you remain in this state of imbalance, the greater the chance of feeling depressed. It may be due to the lack of homeostasis of your estrogen levels or the increased vasomotor symptoms or additional social stressors, or a combination of all these factors. Whatever the reason, the longer you are in flux, the greater may be your risk for depression.

What does this mean in reality? Let's look at Jennifer again. She is forty-four years old. Most likely she has been experiencing these symptoms for three to four years, yet she might not become postmenopausal until the age of fifty-one, like most women. That would mean that she might experience symptoms for ten to eleven years. A decade of declining estrogen, debilitating physical symptoms, and the stress of her everyday life would certainly put her at greater risk for a major depressive episode.

On the flip side of this extended perimenopause is the immediate menopause that's due to surgery. Dr. Shoupe (1999) reported that women who undergo surgical menopause are at higher risk for depression than those who go through menopause naturally. Mostly likely this increased risk of depression is a result of the dramatic drop in estrogen associated with the removal of the ovaries and/or uterus of women who are surgically menopausal.

Lifestyle Choices

There is also some indication that smokers and those who lack physical activity are also at a greater risk for both psychological and *somatic* (physically based) symptoms of depression, according to a review by Dr. Avis and colleagues (2005). It is also believed that diet might influence the risk for perimenopause symptoms. For example, Japanese women report a much lower rate of hot flashes and depression. This may be due to a healthier lifestyle, including less animal protein, less fat, and more soy in their diet. How is soy related to estrogen and mood? As we learned in chapter 1, a balance of hormones, in particular estrogen, is crucial for stabilizing mood. We currently know that soy has estrogen-modulating effects; in other words, it helps to balance female hormones. We will explore this concept and other natural remedies for menopause in chapter 8.

Life Circumstances

Unlike diet and exercise, which can be choices, there are life circumstances beyond our control that increase our chances of becoming depressed. For example, we know that women with a previous history of sexual abuse are at a greater risk for depression. Women who are living at poverty level or have restricted employment/income, along with those who are single mothers, are more likely to experience depression. Those who have a *first-degree relative* (a parent or sibling) with depression are one-and-a-half to three times as likely as others to experience a major depressive episode (APA 1994; Mazure, Keita, and Blehar 2002). In these situations, women do not have much if any control over the circumstances that are affecting their mood issues. But is this related to estrogen? It may be. It is possible that because of their biochemical make-up and their sensitivity to estrogen fluctuations, some women may be more prone to respond to these life circumstances with depression.

Attitudes Toward Menopause

In some circumstances, women do have some control. Drs. Avis and McKinlay (1991) from the Massachusetts Women's Health Study, along with Drs. Woods and Mitchell (1997) from the University of Washington in Seattle, reported that women with a more positive attitude about menopause were less likely to report severe vasomotor symptoms. These researchers speak to the impact of optimism versus pessimism in how a person deals with life's struggles. They also recognize that uncertainty can increase anxiety. Those who are uncertain about what to expect may interpret changes in the body differently than those who have prepared themselves. Be cautious in applying this connection because it may be that women with fewer symptoms are more likely to have a positive attitude about menopause because they are less troubled by hot flashes, and so on. We know that attitudes can influence mood, but we have yet to discover the connection between attitudes and estrogen levels. This is an example of an area that needs further research: what is the interplay between existing estrogen levels, mood functioning, and attitudes or personal perceptions? In the growing investigation of the menopausal transition, there is need for further exploration of mind, body, and environment. One area that has received some attention is the change in cognition that has been associated with menopause and the impact of such change on a women's mood.

Cognitive Changes During Menopause

Dr. Barbara Sherwin from McGill University has been influential in the field of cognition and estrogen. Her initial studies indicated that estrogen deficiency can be associated with lower memory functioning, particularly *verbal memory*, that is, the ability to recall information that is presented orally as opposed to visually (Sherwin 1988, 1990, 1994a, 1994b, 1994c). Even in our own small UCLA study, we found that non-estrogen users (indicating probable estrogen deficiency) performed slightly worse on verbal tasks when compared to estrogen users (Miller et al. 2002). There have been many others who have discussed the link between menopause, estrogen, and cognition. Dr. Sherwin's review of this literature (2003) indicates that there is a belief, not adhered to by all, that estrogen deficiency can cause cognitive decline with age. This concept will be an important one to return to when we talk about treatment and its impact on women.

While most of Dr. Sherwin's work, as with that of other researchers, has focused on cognitive changes during postmenopause, there is a growing awareness that these cognitive changes might be occurring as early as the perimenopausal phase. Postmenopausal women are complaining of cognitive changes, but perimenopausal women are also reporting that they feel more forgetful, less attentive, and have some difficulty with word retrieval. While some of this may be attributed to stress and the normal aging process, there is some evidence suggesting that cognitive changes in perimenopausal women parallel those changes that are well documented in the postmenopausal literature. We recently completed a small pilot study at UCLA to examine this exact issue.

In our study, we set out to explore if there was a distinct cognitive profile for perimenopause. As part of a much larger study with Dr. Gary Small at the UCLA Aging and Memory Research Center, we were able to find a sample of eleven women and eleven men who were matched for age and education. The women were not yet postmenopausal but were reporting significant symptoms of perimenopause. Both men and women were evaluated in terms of cognition and mood. It is important to note that the larger study screened for mood disorders; thus, no one with clinically significant depression or anxiety was included in the smaller study. Having said this, it is not surprising that we found no differences in mood functioning between the women and men. What we did find was that the women were experiencing more difficulty with verbal memory recall. When presented with lists of words or lists of word pairs, the perimenopausal women performed worse than the men. These same women were also experiencing more difficulty with cognitive flexibility, which is typically associated with the frontal lobes in the brain.

While these findings did not focus on significant mood problems, they are certainly related to overall well-being or daily mood functioning. These same women reported that their cognitive changes were stressful and had an impact on how they perceived their ability to function at their jobs. As noted earlier in the chapter, stress and compromised self-perception can be precursors to, that is, can precede depression.

These results were important to us because they actually parallel some of the research on postmenopausal women. While this is certainly a limited study because of the small sample size, it does suggest that verbal memory and difficulties with cognitive flexibility can occur even in the earliest stages of menopause (perimenopause), when we know that estrogen is beginning to decline. We were able to present this research study at both the National Academy of Neuropsychology in Seattle (Miller et al. 2004) and the International Neuropsychological Society in St. Louis (Kernan et al. 2005).

The responses we received at these conferences were very personal. Both women and men, particularly with wives suffering from cognitive complaints in the menopause transition, were interested in more information. These same interested women who were suffering from cognitive changes reported an increase in stress and depression. Based on the responses of professionals and patients, we believe additional exploration of this cognitive profile is warranted, including its impact on social functioning and overall mood state.

Our research is hardly conclusive. We need more studies, larger samples, and measures of actual declining estrogen levels to really understand how cognition and mood changes for perimenopausal women. Furthermore, there are those who embrace the domino theory and believe that memory changes as well as mood symptoms are only secondary to the vasomotor symptoms of menopause. Only future research will be able to tell if declines in attention and memory are directly related to declines in estrogen (or if they are an indirect result of vasomotor symptoms) and how these declines might impact mood.

Conclusion: Reframing Menopause

The majority of the female baby boomer generation, born between 1946 and 1964, are presently experiencing menopause, and many of them are reporting the presence of depression in their lives. Of these thirty-eight million women, approximately thirty million are perimenopausal. This number underscores just how important it is to investigate the menopause transition. The term "perimenopause" did not even come into use until the late 1970s or early 1980s; we've learned a lot since then, but we have a lot yet to learn. This is particularly true in terms of the connection between mood and estrogen during menopause. To date, much of the focus has been on the symptoms of menopause or the social transition, but there is a need for more in-depth exploration of the connection between estrogen and mood during this transitional period of life. Scientific explanations are so incomplete at this time in part because of the variability in research studies. Some studies may include blood levels of estrogen, strict diagnostic criteria for symptoms and mood issues, and a complete evaluation of cognitive functioning; however, most studies include only parts of this information. It is therefore difficult to arrive at decisive comparisons and a conclusion at this time.

As science and technology advance, so will our understanding of the early changes in a woman's estrogen life span. With those advances will come a better understanding of treatment, which we will address in chapters 6, 7, and 8. However, if you are entering into perimenopause or are already postmenopausal and have additional questions or concerns that are beyond the scope of this book, we want you to seek additional information. This chapter on menopause can hardly be comprehensive; there are whole books dedicated to just perimenopause. We have tried to summarize some of the salient aspects of perimenopause and the menopause transition here, including symptoms and associated changes in cognition and mood. For further information, we highly recommend the book *Perimenopause* by Huston and Lanka (2001), which offers an in-depth exploration of the menopausal transition.

It is also important to remember that if you are experiencing some symptoms of menopause, you should have a complete physical exam. This exam should go beyond a gynecological exam and should include an investigation of cardiovascular and neurological systems. In the past, a doctor might have recommended an evaluation of *follicle stimulating hormone* (FSH), but this evaluation is unreliable in the perimenopause phase. The FSH levels may fluctuate month to month and are not always a reliable way to diagnose perimenopause. It is important to note that if you do have your FSH levels tested, do not take the test the day before or during your menstruation when your estrogen levels are naturally at a low point; an FSH test during this time may produce a false reading.

At present, doctors actually find that trial doses of *hormone replacement therapy* (HRT) are more *diagnostic*, that is, they are more definitive in discovering the accurate diagnosis. If a woman responds to a trial dose of HRT and her symptoms improve, it is likely that the symptoms are related to declining estrogen levels. The decision to continue on HRT is one that we will address in chapter 6, the treatment chapter, but it is helpful to know that an initial response to HRT can be a reliable diagnostic tool. Another diagnostic tool might be your own menstrual calendar. Write down when your period arrives as well as the length, flow, and physical or emotional symptoms that you noticed before, during, and after. This information may be helpful in your decision-making process for what treatment, if any, is right for you.

Finally, it is critical to consider your mood functioning in addition to the physical symptoms that you might be experiencing. When getting a complete physical exam, talk to your doctor about your mood and whether or not there are any fluctuations of mood during your cycle. It may be necessary to visit with a psychologist or counselor who is familiar with menopause and how it impacts mood.

It is important to recognize that because women are living longer now—into their eighties—some women will live a third to a half of their lives in the postmenopausal phase. We turn now from the advent to the treatment of menopause, which should be of interest whether you are in menopause now or have yet to make this transition.

CHAPTER 6

Traditional Treatment Approaches

Shelly thought she could handle this menopause transition on her own. She had never been keen on doctors or medicines, and she had basically been healthy her whole life. In fact, her only hospitalization had been for the natural birth of her child thirty years before. Sure, she had suffered from PMS from time to time, but as an avid marathon runner, she got a handle on it by exercising and eating right. Then, at age forty-seven, her periods became irregular, and now, a year later, they were almost nonexistent. She was constantly battling hot flashes and insomnia, and even her hair was falling out. What made it worse was how hard she was hit with depression. A good seven-mile run did not do the trick anymore; it could not snap her out of it. As an advocate of natural solutions, Shelly first turned to the local health food store for help. After researching on the Internet and scanning the store aisles, she selected Saint-John's-wort. Shelly gave it her best shot, trying the herbal remedy for about three months, but it did not seem to help anything. Finally, out of desperation, she visited her family physician, and he recommended hormone replacement therapy. It was against her principles, but she gave it a try. Within three months she felt like herself again, with a new outlook on modern medicine.

Choosing Hormone Replacement Therapy

So far we have spent several chapters discussing the links between estrogen and depression. By now you may be fairly convinced that there is a connection. But understanding the estrogen-depression connection may not be enough. We're guessing that you'll want to know what to do about this mind-body connection. How can someone find relief from the symptoms often associated with an imbalance of estrogen? We recognize that hormone replacement therapy may not be the right choice for all women, but it can be a critically important and beneficial choice for many women.

In this chapter, we will discuss the various types of traditional treatments that might be the right choice for you. In the previous chapters, we have talked about estrogen and progesterone and their unique roles in a woman's body and brain. In this chapter, we will address two types of replacement—*estrogen replacement therapy* (ERT), which typically involves the replacement of estrogen alone, and *hormone replacement therapy* (HRT), which usually involves replacement of both estrogen and progesterone. It's important to keep in mind that in many cases, including in research, the media, and even in your doctor's office, some people use "HRT" to refer to all types of estrogen and/or progesterone replacement.

Depending on your developmental life phase and type of menopause, replacement of estrogen and/or progesterone may be essential to your treatment approach. In addition to describing the types of HRT available, we'll discuss how to approach your doctor and how to individualize your choices to meet your needs. Let's begin with a discussion of estrogen.

Estrogen: Human & Synthetic

First, let's review what kind of estrogens are in the human body so that we have an idea of what is changing or declining with estrogen fluctuation and what might need to be replaced. There are three main types of estrogen in the woman's body:

1. **17-beta estradiol:** Predominant form of estrogen, found throughout the body, influencing over 400 bodily functions

2. **Estrone:** Predominant form of estrogen after menopause, converts to estradiol

3. **Estriol:** Predominant form of estrogen during pregnancy

These are the naturally occurring forms of estrogen, but there are also *synthetic estrogens* available. These are manufactured estrogens that are considered molecularly similar to those produced by your body. Estrace is a manufactured form of 17-beta estradiol, while Ogen and Ortho-Est are forms of estrone. Similar to the estradiol produced by the human body, ethinyl estradiol is also a synthetic estrogen that is most commonly used in birth control but is considered too potent for HRT, thus we do not list it in the table below.

SYNTHETIC SUBSTITUTES FOR HUMAN ESTROGEN
(molecularly the same as human estrogens; obtained from plants)

Human Estrogen	Brand Name of Synthetic
17-beta estradiol	Estrace
Estrone	Ogen or Ortho-Est
Estriol	No substitute commercially available.

Types & Sources of Estrogen

The most common ERT is *conjugated estrogens* (CE), which are derived from pregnant mares' urine, thus the name "Premarin." There are also plant sources of CE, known as Cenestin or Enjuvia. Conjugated estrogens are not a single hormone but a group of several estrogens, which actually may attach to estrogen receptor sites even better than estradiol itself. They also have a prolonged effect, staying in the system for months compared to hours. Menest and Femtrace are not labeled conjugated estrogens, but they are still a mix of several estrogens. Just to clarify, conjugated estrogens and mixed estrogens both include groups of several estrogens.

CONJUGATED & MIXED ESTROGENS

Cenestin

Enjuvia

Femtrace

Menest

Premarin

Non-oral Treatments

Women are using a variety of non-oral methods to treat menopausal symptoms. Both estradiol and CE are available in a *vaginal cream* form. Typically this is used to treat or prevent *atrophy* (thinning) of the vagina, vulva, and bladder. Women who find intercourse painful often seek help with the use of a cream. It can be used in combination with an oral HRT initially or for the long term, depending upon your individual situation. Another non-oral approach is the *vaginal ring*. The primary goal of the vaginal ring is to reverse thinning of the vagina and urinary tract. It is important to note that vaginal creams and rings are targeted to help with atrophy but do not provide significant enough dosage to deliver estrogen to other tissues in the body.

In addition to using a vaginal cream, some women obtain their estradiol replacement via a *skin cream* or *gel*. Skin creams are applied daily to legs, thighs, or calves (e.g., Estrasorb), while skin gels are applied daily to arms (e.g., EstroGel). Many of the pill forms of ERT are also available in cream forms (e.g., Premarin, Estrace), with some of the creams made by compounding pharmacies (e.g., TriEst and BiEst). We will talk more about *compounding* (creating your own HRT with the help of a pharmacist) when we explore alternative approaches to treatment in the coming chapters.

The use of *transdermal patches* is also common. The patch is placed on the skin and releases estrogen continuously. For some, the patch is specifically indicated as the chosen treatment if oral pills have caused side effects such as high blood pressure, nausea, and headaches, or if a woman has any liver complications and needs an alternative to delivery of estrogen through the liver.

CREAMS & GELS

Estrace

Estraderm

Estrasorb

EstroGel

Ogen

Ortho Dienestrol

Premarin

TriEst and BiEst

RINGS & PATCHES

Alora

Climara

Climara Pro

Esclim

Estraderm

Estring

Femring

Menostar

Vivelle-Dot

Designer Estrogens

When we see the word "designer" attached to some product, such as designer jeans, we think that product is somehow superior to others. This concept applies to *designer estrogens* in a limited way. A woman can definitely benefit from designer estrogens. The *selective estrogen receptor modulators* (SERMs) are designed by cellular biologists to deliver estrogen to the selected receptors (like bone receptors) but not to other tissues. This allows a woman to protect her bones without increasing her risk for cancer. The drawback is that these estrogens do not reach the brain, thus they probably do not have an impact on mood or memory. Their job is very specific—to help protect your bones—but other areas of your body could still continue to suffer from the estrogen decline.

Evista (raloxifene) is the most widely used SERM for postmenopausal women as it is targeted to improve bone density but does not increase the risk of cancer. The oldest SERM, Nolvadex (tamoxifen), was designed for both pre- and postmenopausal women with breast cancer. It is also used by women who have no personal history of cancer but are at high risk. In fact, a study in 1998 by Dr. Fisher and colleagues found that women at high risk for breast cancer who used tamoxifen were actually less likely to develop breast cancer when compared to other high-risk women not using tamoxifen. Fareston (toremifene) is relatively new and has only been approved for postmenopausal women with advanced breast cancer. In addition, idoxifene and droloxifene are SERMs that are being studied as tamoxifen *analogues* (additional formulations) to help female cancer patients and possibly to increase bone density in high-risk postmenopausal women.

SERMS

Brand Name	Generic Name
Evista	Raloxifene
Fareston	Toremifene
Nolvadex	Tamoxifen
	Idoxifene
	Droloxifene

Even though our focus is on depression in this book, and SERMs do not yet appear to have an impact on mood, it is important for women to be aware of SERMs as a treatment option, particularly if they are at risk for cancer.

A Combination Approach

As we have discussed throughout this book, it is not estrogen alone that declines with age; there is also an impact on progesterone. It is essential to combine estrogen and progesterone in hormone replacement therapy for women who still have a uterus, to decrease the risk for endometrial cancer. Progesterone protects the uterus because it is an *anti-estrogen* (reduces the action of estrogen within the body), but this also means that it lowers serotonin. Because of this impact, women taking the combination might not feel the same benefit in overall mood functioning as those taking *unopposed estrogen* (estrogen alone).

Discussion of progesterone can be a bit confusing because the terms "progesterone," "progestogen," and "progestins" are often used interchangeably, though not always correctly. *Progesterone* is the human hormone that is produced in the ovaries. The term "progestogen" refers to the wide range of hormones that have properties similar to those of progesterone, including the synthetic compounds called *progestins*.

Both synthetic and natural forms of progesterone are now available, and we list several of these for you in the next table. The benefit of progesterone, beyond endometrial protection, is the lowering of HDL cholesterol. On the flip side, approximately one-third of women may experience side effects from progesterone, including breast tenderness, lower energy level, water retention, increased appetite, bloating, and depression. Synthetic and natural progesterone are available in oral pill, cream, or gel form. (Note that Megace is used primarily in women who are undergoing treatment for cancer and are experiencing hot flashes from tamoxifen use.)

PROGESTOGENS
Amen

Aygestin

Brevicon

Curretab

Cycrin

Megace

Micronor

Mirena

Ovrette

Prochieve

Prometrium

Provera

Some women may take their estrogen and progesterone replacements separately, perhaps one in oral pill form and another in a cream. Others want to take a combination of estrogen and progesterone in one HRT product. The choice is up to the individual, with guidance from her doctor. As mentioned previously, women going through a natural rather than surgical menopause are most likely to take a combination estrogen and progesterone when choosing HRT, in order to decrease their risk of cancer.

COMBINATION TREATMENTS

Activella

Climara Pro

CombiPatch

Estratest

Femhrt

Ortho-Prefest

Premphase

Prempro

Choices

As you can see from the above tables, there are a lot of choices. We have tried to make these lists as complete as possible, but as the pharmaceutical business advances every day, there may be some additional ERT and HRT choices. We felt it would be helpful to list these compounds so that you could discuss them with your doctor. It is critical to think about what feels right to you. In fact, let's meet four women who are friends but have made very different choices in their approach to treating menopause, its symptoms, and depression.

Michelle, Anne, Christy, and Darlene met years ago as new moms. Over time, they managed to keep in touch, arrange playdates for the kids, and eventually have just-girls dinners. Fifteen years after having their kids, they are going through a new phase together—menopause. Each describes the process a little differently, but all agree that there has been a change in their moods, with more irritability on a daily basis and more propensity for depressive episodes. What is dramatically different about these women are the choices they have made during their transition into menopause. Michelle has a family history of breast cancer, with her aunt dying at age fifty and her mom being a current survivor. She opted to use a SERM, Evista, to address her menopausal concerns. Anne recently suffered from uncontrollable heavy bleeding, and her doctor recommended a complete hysterectomy. After receiving a second opinion, she had the surgery and took her doctor's advice to start on Premarin. Christy is just beginning to experience perimenopausal symptoms and tends to have a minimalist approach to treatment. Because intercourse has been painful with her partner, she decided to use a vaginal cream but is not taking another form of HRT at this time. Finally, Darlene is quick to complain about the host of menopausal symptoms that she is experiencing as natural menopause progresses in her life. Darlene decided to take Prempro in order to have a strong delivery of estrogen but also for the protection of progesterone. These four women exemplify a few of the many choices or combinations that women might consider in their approach to treating estrogen deficiency. What these four stories do not tell you is that it is not all about the female hormones. Male hormones play a role in the overall health of a woman as well.

Male Hormones

Women have both estrogens and *androgens* (male hormones), including *testosterone* and *androstenedione*. From puberty to menopause, women have a relatively stable ratio of estrogens to androgens, with significantly higher estrogen levels. When this ratio becomes unbalanced, for example, when estrogen declines in menopause, androgens are no longer suppressed and "male-like" physical characteristics may emerge, including facial hair and a deeper voice. There is also a change in fat distribution, with more fat settling around the abdomen than the hips and thighs (resulting in more of an apple- than a pear-shaped body). Also, male hormones are important for energy, muscle tissue, bones, and the brain, but as the ovaries shut down there is a possible deficiency in androgens, which may result in the following: loss of muscle mass (as in flabby arms, for example), poor attention span, decreased interest in sex, dry skin, or thinning hair.

When women have gone through surgical menopause, both the estrogen and androgen levels drop, and a combination of estrogen and male hormone replacement may be indicated. This may also be true if there is a significant loss of interest in sex or very low energy levels. Finally, those with osteoporosis and compression fractures can also benefit from adding testosterone to HRT or ERT.

At this point, it is also important to address *dehydroepiandrosterone* (DHEA), which is also an androgen and is produced by the adrenal gland. This is considered a weak androgen that has some impact on aging and is known to decline across the life span. The role of DHEA on mood, memory, and overall functioning is not well understood. The impact of DHEA to improve mood and memory is documented by some, but there is some controversy as to whether or not DHEA would be beneficial as a treatment for mood or memory problems (Barnhart et al. 1999; Dayal et al. 2005). Despite these unclear results, Dr. Genazzani and colleagues (2003) found that DHEA supplementation increased hormone levels in postmenopausal women and reduced menopause symptoms, suggesting that use of DHEA may be an alternative to HRT. In reviewing the impact of DHEA, Dr. Santoro and colleagues (2005) explained that while there appears to be a link between DHEA and mood, it is unclear if the link is a direct cause and effect. We look to future research that may be able to tell us if DHEA replacement will be beneficial to women for treating depression.

An Alternative: Antidepressants

Whether just estrogen or a combination of hormones, HRT might not be an appropriate choice for some women. A woman might choose not to use HRT because of family or personal medical history, or just because of a personal concern about synthetic hormones. On the flip side, for some women HRT might not be enough to battle the symptoms of menopause, including depression. It may therefore be a better option for some to take an antidepressant. In fact, for some women, it is necessary to take a combination of HRT and an antidepressant. There is a strong agreement both in research and in the clinical field that selective serotonin reuptake inhibitors (SSRIs) are the best approach for most women who are suffering from depression connected to estrogen changes, whether it is related to the onset of puberty, postpartum depression, or menopause. While there are other antidepressants available that are certainly effective for treating all kinds of depression, women seem to respond better to an SSRI perhaps because of the connection between estrogen and serotonin. We described this connection in chapter 1. If our brains need the right levels of serotonin to balance our mood, and declining levels of estrogen can upset that balance, it may be necessary to re-create that balance using an SSRI.

In the past, the SSRIs prescribed were those that might also be prescribed to men and women presenting with depression that did not necessarily have an estrogen connection. Now doctors, researchers, and pharmaceutical companies are trying to tailor medication to specific disorders. For example, Sarafem (fluoxetine hydrochloride) is touted as a treatment for premenstrual dysphoric disorder, which we discussed in chapter 3. Common examples of SSRIs are listed below by both brand name and generic name. The choice for you may depend on the depressive symptoms you present. It is also important to keep in mind that each person's brain chemistry is a little different. It may take trying two or three medications, while consulting your doctor, before the right one for you can take effect. This requires flexibility, patience, and sometimes a combination of other lifestyle changes or interventions, which we will discuss in chapter 8.

SELECTIVE SEROTONIN REUPTAKE INHIBITORS (SSRIS)

Brand Name	Generic Name
Celexa	Citalopram
Effexor	Venlafaxine
Lexapro	Escitalopram oxalate
Paxil	Paroxetine
Prozac	Fluoxetine
Sarafem	Fluoxetine hydrochloride
Zoloft	Sertraline

NOTE: *In this chapter we attempted to give our readers a fairly comprehensive list of estrogen and progesterone replacement therapies in addition to some antidepressants, but the lists and chapter are not exhaustive and some other medications may exist. Therefore, we strongly suggest that you consult your physician regarding the best possible choice for you.*

Seeking Treatment

So far we have focused on the traditional treatment approaches to estrogen and progesterone replacement therapy. Hopefully these lists will help you to be better informed in your own decisions. Next, let's talk about how to approach the right treatment for you.

First, you want to consider your family history and medical history. It might help to write these histories down so that you will have it organized for your physician. Do you have any family history of cancer, heart disease, strokes, or osteoporosis? If so, write down the type of medical issue and the relative that it has impacted. These may represent genetic risk factors for you.

Next, let's take into consideration your own medical history. Do you have a history of diabetes, hypertension, obesity, heart problems, vascular-related changes, high cholesterol, or seizures? What medications are you currently taking? If you are going to see a new physician, it is helpful to have copies of your old medical records.

You will also want to consider your individual psychological history. Are there any previous mood issues, such as anxiety, depression, or irritability during your life span? Is there any history of PMS, PMDD, or postpartum depression? What do these mood issues seem to be connected to? Do you have a history of family problems, trauma, or difficulty with relationships? Do you feel that any of your mood symptoms coincide with periods of estrogen fluctuation, such as puberty, PMS, pregnancy, or menopause?

Next, you will want to consider your current physical and mental state. Are you able to determine if you are perimenopausal, or, perhaps, menopausal? What are your symptoms, and which ones are the most bothersome? Do any of the symptoms seem to be getting worse with time? How is your mood state?

How would you rate your anxiety or depression? Do you feel it is impacting your ability to function in relationships or at work?

Finally, what are your feelings about estrogen or hormone replacement therapy? What are the questions and concerns that you'd like to address with the doctor? Are there certain side effects you are worried about? Have you thought about what approach would be best for you, given your medical and psychological history?

After you have filled up a few pages with your own history, you will be better prepared to approach your physician and ask about what treatment might be best for you. Here is a brief guide to approaching your physician for the right formula for you.

- Discuss your *chief complaint* or main symptoms. State which symptoms bother you most.

- Discuss how the symptoms might also relate to your *current medical issues* and medications.

- Be sure to address your *psychological issues.* Be open about your feelings and overall mood state.

- Explain your own *medical history* and *family history* to the physician. This is necessary, even if you feel this doctor knows you well. Remember that physicians see hundreds of patients, and while they may recall your current medical status, they often need reminding about your past and certainly about your family history.

- Ask the physician about *treatment options.* Now is the time to address what you are looking for, which may be immediate symptom relief or a long-term interest in overall protection from estrogen loss.

- Address your *concerns and questions.* If you have them written down, you are less likely to forget to ask them, and it will be helpful to take the time to write down some of the doctor's answers.

In the end, if you are not satisfied with the answers that your doctor provides regarding your personal list of symptoms and medical history, you feel your doctor is not knowledgeable (they should know most of the information in this book), or you feel your doctor is not listening to you or is unable to consider an individualized treatment plan for you, you may need to seek two or three opinions. It might take visiting several physicians before you find someone knowledgeable about the estrogen-related changes that occur with menopause and to find the ideal and individualized treatment approach for you. Remember, you are the expert on your body, your feelings, and what you need. If you feel that your physician is not listening to your complaints and is not offering you relief from your symptoms, seek another opinion.

Let's see how this guide is used in a real-world situation. Judith is perimenopausal and has been having irregular periods for almost two years. Initially, she did not think to seek any type of medical help for her symptoms. She figured the symptoms would remain mild, and besides she was just too busy to see the doctor. Then she read the brief guide listed above and realized she really should put her history down on paper and think about her current symptoms. Since she had recently switched jobs and insurance companies, her current internist didn't know her very well. First, Judith took about an hour to jot down all of her history as well as her current symptoms, and then she visited her physician.

Upon meeting Dr. Kim, she knew she was going to be comfortable talking about these personal issues. Dr. Kim had an easygoing demeanor and was quick to give Judith a smile. Plus Judith guessed they were around the same age. Dr. Kim listened intently as Judith talked about her mother's history of cancer as well as her own history of migraine headaches and high blood pressure. Then Judith talked about her menopausal symptoms, including the hot flashes and the significant depression that seemed to be impacting her marriage and her ability to function well at work. Dr. Kim asked about possible androgen-deficit-related symptoms, like a decline in sex drive or a thinning of hair. Surprised, Judith noted these symptoms as well. Dr. Kim then confirmed that it had been a while since Judith had had any type of physical exam. Dr. Kim initially recommended Prempro, a combination of estrogen and progesterone. Dr. Kim carefully explained that there is little increased risk for cancer associated with short-term use of HRT. But Judith was reluctant to consider this approach after becoming teary-eyed while describing her mother's battle with breast cancer. After much discussion, Dr. Kim and Judith agreed that they would do a full blood panel, including looking at hormone levels. Since Judith's mood was most disturbing to her and because of her family history of cancer, they decided that at first they would try an SSRI antidepressant for the mood issues as well as natural supplements to address the hot flashes. After about six months, they would review her progress and think about her satisfaction with this treatment approach.

Judith's impression was that Dr. Kim was open, knowledgeable, and took the time to think about different treatment approaches. They were able to arrive at an individualized approach to Judith's menopausal situation and symptoms. Sometimes it will take visiting several doctors to achieve this kind of interaction and plan, but when armed with the information you have learned in this book, you are likely to achieve the right answer for you.

Conclusion

You can see that there are many possible choices for estrogen and progesterone use. Many women may feel like many of their symptoms are natural and therefore should simply be accepted. Their mothers may not have pursued treatment, or they may feel as though they should simply endure a host of menopausal symptoms. But it is important for their health and quality of life to consider how treatment might be beneficial. When thinking about treatment, it is critical to consider your own personal medical history and that of your family when consulting your doctor for the right medication. Some women will be at greater risk for certain types of cancer, like breast cancer, if their mother or grandmother was diagnosed with the same. If this applies to you, you might want to consider alternative treatments, which we are going to discuss in the chapters to come. Finally, before making a decision as to whether HRT is right for you, you may want to better understand both the benefits and risks of HRT, including its impact on your brain, which we will discuss in chapter 7. Armed with the long lists of possible HRT approaches, a guide to approaching your doctor, and the well-balanced picture of benefits and risks, you will be better prepared to make your individual decision regarding HRT and how it may be important to address your own estrogen-depression connection. Next we will explore how HRT impacts not only mood functioning, but also a woman's cognition, and we will address the risks associated with HRT.

CHAPTER 7

Impact of Traditional Treatment

Remember Joan and Jean from chapter 5? They were the sisters who experienced the transition of menopause in very different ways, yet had a similar reaction—sadness. Joan went through menopause naturally, while Jean required a complete hysterectomy. Their choices of treatment and the impact of those treatments were also dramatically different. As we learned in the last chapter, traditional choices for treatment of postmenopausal symptoms, including depression, can vary depending upon what type of menopause a woman experiences. As Joan was going through natural menopause, she was hit by significant depression and decided that she should try a combination of estrogen and progesterone replacement therapy. Within just a few weeks after starting the traditional approach of using Prempro, Joan began to enjoy life again. She resumed planning her cruise around the world and finally delighted in being a grandmother.

Jean's journey of treatment was a bit more difficult. At her doctor's suggestion, she finally tried Premarin and did feel some relief from her postmenopausal symptoms, experiencing fewer hot flashes and better sleep. But the blues still hung around. After another six months of feeling discouraged to the point that she did not want to talk on the phone to her sister who seemed to be handling "the change of life" so well, Jean finally decided to consult her doctor again. Her doctor suggested that HRT was not enough; perhaps she should also try an antidepressant and short-term therapy. Within six weeks of taking Prozac, Jean felt dramatically better, ready to take on the world again, and even considered joining her sister for that cruise around the world. Jean also found psychotherapy to be extremely helpful as she realized that while many of her depressive symptoms could be attributed to the estrogen-depression link, there were also some life issues she had been ignoring.

Do all women have such success stories with hormone replacement therapy (HRT) and the use of antidepressants? We know each woman is different, as is her response to HRT and other medications. However, there is a strong link between depression and declining estrogen levels, and this has been supported for the most part by the research that explores the successful impact of HRT on mood functioning in postmenopausal women.

First, let's examine the approach and success of treating clinical depression in postmenopausal women. Next, we will consider the impact of HRT on nondepressed women, who may report some symptoms of depression but don't meet enough of the criteria to have a formal diagnosis of depression. We will explore how HRT improves their mood functioning. Our information comes mainly from three sources: research designed in an experimental setting (where the treatment can be manipulated), observational research (where women choose their own treatment), and case examples from our clients, friends, and colleagues.

Assessing treatment options is complex because depression is complex. As we discussed in earlier chapters, depression can come from multiple sources, and the link between estrogen and depression can depend on, and be mediated by, multiple factors. Any one treatment is therefore unlikely to work for every woman. However, estrogen treatment has emerged as an effective and viable treatment option that should be considered. What follows are some helpful generalities to consider.

Depressed Postmenopausal Women

Postmenopausal depression can be the most difficult type of depression to treat because the estrogen deficiency may decrease the responsiveness of serotonin-based antidepressants, such as Prozac and Zoloft (Joffe and Cohen

1998; Schneider, Small, and Clary 2001). In other words, not only are post-menopausal women at greater risk for depression, probably due to the very low levels of estrogen, but the medications used to treat depression may also be less effective in this stage. Because HRT can improve symptoms of depression and enhance the efficacy of antidepressants, a combination may be necessary to treat depression in some postmenopausal women (Zec and Trivedi 2002). Dr. Schneider and associates (2001) found that this combination was success-ful in at least 20 percent of the women they studied. The women in their study improved in the number and severity of depressive symptoms. For example, a woman with moderate depression, who reports daily sadness, frequent insom-nia, anxious mood, and several aches and pains, may later report less frequent depression and anxiety, improved sleep, and less physical discomfort after taking HRT and antidepressants. In Dr. Schneider's study, this improvement was less certain if the woman was taking only HRT or only an antidepressant. It was the combination that was critical to overall improvement in mood.

This combination is not for everyone. In fact, there are some research-ers who have not detected any antidepressant effects from HRT (Hays et al. 2003; Morrison et al. 2004). It is truly difficult to draw conclusions because of the heterogeneity of research studies; in others words, there are often many different approaches to studying this connection, and these studies yield a range of results. For example, we do not yet have a good understanding of whether HRT has a different effect on depression for women who go through menopause naturally as opposed to those who are surgically menopausal. Much of the research to date has included both types of women in their studies. Because both have been included in the studies, the type of HRT has also varied. With so much variation in studies, the information we receive is hardly conclusive, but it does begin to suggest a trend.

Sometimes HRT is not a viable option to treat depression in women, but use of an antidepressant, like an SSRI, is a good choice. In chapter 6 we listed commonly prescribed SSRI medications, like Prozac. Antidepressants are a well-established treatment for menopausal women, alleviating depression and often symptoms like hot flashes (Soares, Poitras, and Prouty 2003; Cohen, Soares, and Joffe 2005). Typically, women feel an improvement in their mood within one month, and overall wellness is typically achieved if the woman remains on the antidepressant for at least six to twelve months.

To fully understand the personal impact of major depression in the post-menopausal phase, let's look at Shirley's experience. We first met Shirley at a community talk. After hearing about the risks of depression in postmeno-pause, she came up to us and described her current situation. She had recently retired after teaching school for forty years. She was not sleeping well, had no appetite, felt guilty for not being a "productive member of society," and was struggling to make plans with friends and family for social dates. The worst of it, she said, was that after all these years, she felt as if life was not really worth living. Despite her strong religious beliefs, she was having constant thoughts about driving her car off a cliff or overdosing on pain medication. She was struggling to find meaning in her new life as a retired, single person. After hearing our talk, she decided to seek out some additional answers.

In the initial therapy session, Shirley reported that she had a history of PMS, had experienced postpartum depression, and had been postmenopausal for about two years. Medically, she never really addressed her PMS, and her postpartum depression had been complicated by the death of her infant and husband within a year of her child's birth. Shirley's work ethic and the con-stant support of her church community had been the foundation of her recov-ery process thirty years earlier. After hearing about the depression-estrogen connection, she better understood that her history of depression put her at risk for another cycle of major depression during menopause. We recom-mended that she receive a medication consultation from a geriatric psychia-trist with the hope that a combination of HRT and an antidepressant would bring symptom relief. We also continued to have Shirley participate in weekly psychotherapy over the next year to address life changes, such as retirement, and to process unresolved grief issues surrounding the death of her husband and infant. Within one year, Shirley was able to happily proclaim that she was not depressed. In fact, she was feeling vibrant and reported that she was now involved in several community activities and socially engaged with new and old friends.

An Experiment: Estrogen's Link to Well-Being

You may know someone in menopause who isn't diagnosed with depression, and you might wonder if estrogen only plays a role in mood for those women who are depressed. Or does it have a significant role in mood for women who are not clinically depressed? As we have learned in this book, estrogen certainly can influence mood, but not all women become depressed just because they have fluctuations in estrogen levels. Likewise, not all postmenopausal women become depressed. What does this mean about the role of estrogen in the nondepressed, postmenopausal woman?

Estrogen still appears to be important for women who do not develop depression during the postmenopausal years. Even if a woman is not diagnosed with depression, she may still be experiencing some depressive symptoms during the menopause transition.

We know this by examining the experiments conducted on postmenopausal women who were not clinically depressed. Several studies support this notion. Drs. Zweifel and O'Brien (1997) conducted a meta-analysis, which is a mathematical computation where the data from several studies with the same focus are examined. They reported that 76 percent of HRT users had lower depression scores than the nonusers. Keep in mind that these women were not clinically depressed but may have shown some symptoms of depression. In this review, they found that more women taking unopposed ERT had lower depression scores than those using a combination of progesterone and estrogen. But the women taking a combination of HRT still had lower depression scores than the nonusers (control subjects).

A few years ago we were asked to review all the past and current literature on this subject (Miller 2003). We found ten experimental research studies suggesting that women taking HRT self-report that they have less depressive symptoms (for example, have better well-being) when compared to women not taking HRT. In contrast, eight different studies suggested no such relationship. Once again, it is hard to make conclusive statements because the research studies vary significantly in terms of the women they include and the type of estrogen being used by these women. Having said that, we lean more toward the positive effects of HRT on mood symptoms, based on the meta-analysis of Drs. Zweifel and O'Brien (1997), the review of literature conducted by Drs. Zec and Trivedi (2002), and an impressive study by Dr. Hlatky and colleagues (2002). In this latter study, 2,763 postmenopausal women were *randomized*, or randomly directed into treatment either with HRT or with a placebo (that is, no treatment but a "sugar pill" was given). In their findings, the women who had significant menopausal symptoms, like hot flashes, were also likely to show improvement in their mood and overall quality of life. This improvement was significant for those taking HRT. The work of Dr. Hlatky and colleagues suggests that HRT should be considered a first-line treatment if a postmenopausal woman is demonstrating signs of vasomotor symptoms and depression.

What might a woman in these experimental studies look like? Sally, a sixty-three-year-old postmenopausal woman, decided she wanted more information about this estrogen business and heard about a research study at her local university. The study was interesting to her because she would get a free evaluation, including a physical exam, a full blood panel, and an assessment of her mood. This seemed worthwhile to her because she did not have medical insurance, was too young to qualify for Medicare, and was concerned about her mood. She did not think that she had major depression, at least the way these doctors were describing it, but she certainly felt blue at times, down on herself, and then there were a host of postmenopausal symptoms. The symptoms that bothered her the most were the hot flashes, her low sex drive, and her inability to get a good night's sleep. After signing up for the research study and completing the initial exams, she met with the clinical research nurse. The nurse gave her a bottle of unmarked pills and explained that she might be receiving the HRT treatment or that these pills might be placebos, which are essentially nothing but a sugar pill that would have no effect on her system.

After just one week, Sally noticed a dramatic change in her physical symptoms, including fewer hot flashes and more restful sleep. She was sure that she was on the real thing! In a few weeks, her overall mood was better. There were less days of feeling blue, and she realized that she was less irritable, and more likely to have kind words for her husband or neighbors. The research study concluded in three months and the "blind" was broken, meaning that the researchers could tell the participants whether they were on HRT or the placebo. Sally, indeed, had been on HRT. She felt so good about the results and her new self that she went to her doctor to continue her prescription.

Sally's experience and the actual results of experimental research studies suggest a definitive link between estrogen and depression in postmenopausal women. This link appears to be present and strong, even in women who are not clinically depressed. From this we can suggest that each woman's menopausal profile should be considered carefully in terms of type of menopause, associated symptoms, and appropriate use of HRT. This is true not only for women within an experimental setting, but also borne out by the observations of women within a natural environment of self-prescribed choices. We will discuss this approach with more depth, later in the chapter.

An Observation: Estrogen's Link to Well-Being

So far we have suggested that there is a definite link between estrogen deficiency and depression in women who appear clinically depressed, along with a connection between HRT and improved depressive symptoms in nondepressed women within an experimental setting. What about women who are not depressed and who are not in some type of experimental research study? Some of the strongest evidence for understanding the estrogen-depression connection in postmenopausal women comes from observing just such women.

In the research world, there are several types of study designs. The "ideal" study is thought to be an experimental study in which you can assign some people to a treatment and some people to a placebo or no treatment. This is not always a realistic way to study people and the effects of life choices. Because many people do not want their choices made for them, experimental studies are often small (in terms of number of subjects). In contrast, many people are willing to help science out by offering their information willingly by taking written tests (like memory tasks) or talking to doctors and even answering questions about their mood. But they do not want to be told what medication to take or not to take. We can learn a lot about people from these types of observational studies. Some of the most important information about estrogen and depression has come from this type of study.

Within these observational studies, we notice that surgically-induced menopausal women are more likely to use HRT, particularly unopposed estrogen. These same women often report less depression. Remember that we mentioned earlier a review study we did a few years ago? We also examined observational research studies that reported a positive association between HRT and mood in nondepressed women (Miller 2003). One of these studies was our own, conducted at UCLA (Miller et al. 2002). Our study was unique in that it examined both women and men in terms of their mood. We had three groups of people: males, female postmenopausal HRT users, and female postmenopausal non-HRT users. We had all of them complete a self-report questionnaire where we asked them questions about their mood, including questions about depression, anger, anxiety, and vigor (feeling energetic). The HRT users reported less depression and less anger than both the non-HRT users and the men. We believe that this was an important finding for under-standing the estrogen-depression connection. Women taking HRT are going to have more estrogen surging in their brain than men or women not taking HRT. If the HRT users are reporting better mood, including less depression and anger than others, then we have a better understanding about the impor-tance of estrogen for maintaining mood functioning during the menopausal years.

These observational studies also offer us an important perspective on the importance of time. Experimental studies are often conducted during perimenopause or the initial postmenopausal phase, and may last only a few months to two to three years. In contrast, observational studies are usually lon-gitudinal in that they continue for many years after menopause has occurred. The results of observational studies are less likely to concentrate on relief of acute symptoms of depression and are more likely to measure *overall well-being* or positive mood. Thus, the results often implicate "better mood" for HRT users, as compared to an actual improvement in depression. A review in 2002 reported that over 50 percent of the observational studies indicate that HRT is associated with significantly higher scores on general mood (Zec and Trivedi 2002). In 2003, our review found that 70 percent of the observational studies indicated better mood functioning and well-being for HRT users.

Unlike her neighbor Sally, who had signed up for the experimental research study we mentioned earlier, Dorothy was not about to have someone gamble with her life and give her some unknown medication or a sugar pill. Dorothy had had a hysterectomy early in life because of endometriosis. As a result, she began taking Premarin, which, you may recall from earlier discussion, is a type of unopposed estrogen replacement therapy. Now, twenty years later, Dorothy was somewhat concerned about her brain. She wanted to know about the impact of HRT on her memory and mood, and how she was aging relative to her peers.

After hearing a radio advertisement for a research study, she agreed to a full evaluation of her mood and memory functioning in addition to providing information about medical history. The researchers explained that this was an observational study with no medication or placebo involved. This felt like a good fit for Dorothy because she wanted to contribute to science and wanted additional information about her memory, but she did not want to change her medication regimen. The research study ended up giving Dorothy good news, telling her that her memory was similar to others her age and that her mood did not seem to be impacting her overall functioning. It was even possible that HRT provided some protection for her brain, including her cognition and mood.

Dorothy's case shows that observational research might be attracting a certain group of women that want to be in studies. In research, some say there is a *healthy user bias*, meaning that observational studies recruit women who are more health conscious and who may be doing several things that result in better health and mood (that is, diet, exercise, medical check-ups, and so on). Also, many of these observational studies include both unopposed and combination HRT users, so we are less clear about how HRT influences women with natural menopause (who typically use combination HRT) versus women with surgical menopause (who typically use unopposed HRT). In contrast to our assessment of Dr. Zweifel's study that we mentioned earlier, it is not clear whether or not those taking a combination of estrogen and progesterone have less improvement in mood than those taking just estrogen alone. In the studies we have mentioned, there has not been a significant difference in the inclusion or exclusion of the combination users in analyses of the sample population (Kimura 1995; Sherwin 1998; Maki, Zonderman, and Resnick 2001). This holds true for our own research as well (Miller et al. 2002; Miller 2003). Progesterone has also been considered when observing mood enhancement in postmenopausal women because there is some controversy as to whether or not progesterone reduces the effects of estrogen on mood (Archer 1999; Cummings and Brizendine 2002).

Summing It Up

With all these possible combinations, it is hard to be certain what science is telling us. There are experimental and observational studies, and there are studies that include postmenopausal women with and without clinical depression. Perhaps the best information on the big picture comes from the researchers who conduct review studies or meta-analyses because they want to get to the bottom of the mystery. In other words, they want to sum it up for us.

In 1995, Dr. Pearce and associates attempted one of the first review studies. Out of 111 studies on postmenopausal women, only a few of those articles actually addressed the mood issue. When just looking at women who had gone through natural menopause, they found no consistent association between HRT and improvement for depression. Why does mood improve for some women taking a combination of estrogen and progesterone, but not for others? It is possible that one of the mediating factors is that progesterone can dampen estrogen's ability to enhance mood. These findings were in contrast to those for the surgically menopausal women, who faired better in terms of "well-being" or overall elevated mood. The review did notice that the more positive results were likely to come from observational studies rather than from experimental studies, where the results were more mixed. They summed it up by stating that at least 67 percent of the reviewed studies associated HRT with mood improvement.

A few years later, Drs. Zweifel and O'Brien (1997) published a meta-analysis of twenty-six HRT studies that statisticians and researchers felt were well-designed and well-executed studies with enough subjects to produce meaningful results. The conclusions were very positive in terms of HRT and mood. Similar to previous results, they reported the most meaningful connection between unopposed estrogen and a reduction in depressed mood, with approximately 76 percent of HRT users demonstrating lower depression scores than nonusers. Next came combinations of estrogen and progesterone, which also resulted in mood improvement as did combinations of androgen and estrogen. However, the meaningful connections were smaller in progesterone and androgen studies than in unopposed estrogen studies, suggesting that a little less than 50 percent may have demonstrated lower depression scores compared to those not taking the medication. Their review included both nondepressed and depressed women. The connection between HRT and better mood can be generalized most to women with depression or mild depressive symptoms. This further suggests a strong link between estrogen deficiency and depression in postmenopausal women. It also points to the importance of HRT for these women.

In 2001, Drs. Soares and Cohen took a slightly different approach. They suggested that there are three types of study conclusions examining the influence of estrogen on depression. First, there are studies that find no association between HRT and improvement in women's mood. Second, there are studies that suggest estrogen as *monotherapy* (meaning the use of estrogen alone) for depression. These studies report that estrogen alone can improve the mood of clinically depressed women. Third, there are studies that suggest that HRT in conjunction with an antidepressant may improve a woman's mood, quality of life, and health.

In thinking about Drs. Soares and Cohen's study, we might speculate that the first group of women, who did not improve with HRT, have a complex presentation of depression. Estrogen deficiency may only be one aspect of their depression profile. Other factors, such as long-term family or relationship issues, personality factors, and environmental situations, may be the more critical factors affecting their mood functioning. In the second group, the cause of depression might be directly linked to estrogen deficiency, making monotherapy HRT sufficient to improve mood. This group supports what we learned in chapter 1 about brain chemistry and mood. Finally, the last group, where a combination of HRT and antidepressants works best, speaks to estrogen's role in facilitating the serotonergic aspects of antidepressants. Remember from chapter 1 that a deficiency of serotonin is the reigning theory about the biological cause of depression. Without estrogen, antidepressants cannot do their job in some women.

We were asked in 2003 to do an additional review of the postmenopausal estrogen literature. As part of an invited review for *Current Psychiatry Reports*, we examined mood improvement and HRT in twenty-seven studies for nondepressed women (fourteen experimental studies and thirteen observational) and twenty-one articles that addressed HRT and mood improvement in depressed women. Four articles that were reviews or meta-analyses were also considered, as well as research on the mood of women compared to the mood of men. Within this review, we concluded that experimental studies for nondepressed women offer no clear evidence for mood improvement associated with HRT because 50 percent reported no significant findings. The observational studies were a different story. In observational studies of nondepressed women, there was a stronger association between mood improvement and HRT. Finally, there was moderate evidence that HRT also facilitates the improvement of clinical depression, including the efficacy of antidepressants.

Bottom Line

What does all this mean? Basically, it means that there are several factors to consider when trying to understand and assess study results. Experimental studies might give researchers more control over the design and possibly the outcomes of their studies, but they are also short-term studies, ranging from only a few weeks to five years in duration. Five years may seem like a lot, but it only gives us a brief window into the short-term impact of HRT on mood and other aspects of brain functioning. On the flip side, observational studies allow women to make their own choices, including whether or not to use HRT. It also allows women to engage in a healthy lifestyle of their own choosing. Sure, it might be harder to draw generalizations from observations of this type of woman, but real life is about making your own choices. What we think is important is that given that women are typically taking HRT for longer periods of time, maybe five to twenty years, observational studies help us find out how long-term use of HRT might impact overall mood and memory.

The contrast between these two types of studies (experimental and observational) is a key to understanding the current debate about HRT use. It may not even be possible to observe the full impact of the estrogen-depression connection within a short window of time; the connection may need to be observed over the span of a woman's lifetime, from puberty to menopause, including several years, if not decades, after menopause—something an observational study can do. And the overall impact of HRT is also difficult to gauge within the short time period of an experimental study. However, the immediate impact of HRT on mood can be understood within an experimental study. This leads us to believe that the most useful conclusions can be drawn by looking at postmenopausal women within both the short- and long-term frameworks.

Impact on the Brain

When looking at this research, particularly in the context of the personal choice as to whether or not HRT is right for you, it is important to consider the influence of HRT on the brain and cognitive functioning. Consider four concepts:

1. Some researchers have been able to establish a link between better memory and HRT use.

2. The impact of HRT on the brain may be a matter of timing.

3. Women taking HRT might be less at risk for developing dementia.

4. HRT users have brains that are different from those of nonusers, in that they may have more efficient brains (as measured by metabolic activity).

If a depressed woman is thinking about HRT but isn't sure if it's the best option for her, this additional information might just be the encouragement she needs to find out if HRT is the right choice. In chapter 1, we talked about how our brains govern our mood functioning at the biochemical level. Because of this connection between mood and the brain, it is helpful to explore how HRT is influencing our brain. We also know that memory and mood are connected in many ways. If we are depressed, we may not feel like our memory is as accurate. If we are upset about our memory abilities, we might feel depressed. If we recall upsetting memories, we might also feel depressed. If we are in a better mood, we are more likely to feel as though our memory is working better. With these links in mind, let's take a look at these four important concepts.

Better Memory

As we discussed in chapter 1, there is a high concentration of estrogen receptors in the brain, so it is no surprise that HRT might improve brain performance. This seems particularly true for attention and concentration in addition to *verbal memory* (recalling information that is presented verbally). Dr. Barbara Sherwin and colleagues (1988, 1994a, 1994b, 1994c) have published several articles that suggest a connection between improvement of memory with HRT. Others have also made similar claims (Henderson, Watt, and Buckwalter 1996; Wolf et al. 1999; Le Blanc et al. 2001). Since the *hippocampus* (the memory center) in the brain has a high number of estrogen receptors, it makes sense that declining estrogen might have an impact on memory. It also makes sense that replacing the declining estrogen would be essential for maintaining memory functioning.

It is also possible that estrogen replacement has a direct impact on attention and concentration (Carlson and Sherwin 1998; Duff and Hampson 2000). In our own research study at UCLA, we found that women taking HRT had better attention and *verbal fluency*, or the ability to retrieve words, as compared to women not taking HRT (Miller et al. 2002). We also found a trend that women taking HRT had better memory scores when compared to those not taking HRT. Is there a direct link in the brain between estrogen and attentiveness? Or does HRT improve menopausal symptoms, which, in turn, allows women to be more attentive? This question of cause and effect reminds us of the domino theory that we discussed in chapter 5. But more recent brain imaging indicates the possible direct effect of ERT on the brain. When compared to non-ERT users, the women given ERT had better brain efficiency, that is, they had better sustained attention and had an increased response in several regions of the brain (Stevens, Clark, and Prestwood 2005).

Despite the findings of our own research and the research of several others, one recent meta-analysis highlights the overall inconsistency in the research on HRT's impact on cognition (memory, attention, and so on). Based on these results, the researchers suggest that there is no real benefit from HRT on cognition (Low and Anstey 2006). However, caution should be applied because their conclusions are only based on 22 out of a possible 105 research studies on HRT and cognition. What their article really highlights is that there is no clear, uniform answer regarding the impact of HRT on memory. In addition, the outcomes of many research studies are most likely impacted by the timing of HRT use in the menopause phase.

Timing

The old phrase "timing is everything" appears to be key to the connection between HRT and cognition. This means that studies that found no impact of HRT on cognition are not necessarily conclusive. Cutting-edge neuroscientists are just learning that the timing of estrogen delivery might be a contributing factor when trying to determine whether HRT improves memory or not. Zhao and colleagues (2005) have begun developing models of cells showing that the delivery of estrogen to the hippocampus prior to any *atrophy* (damage as a result of aging) can result in better survival of brain cells. This effect was not observed when estrogen was delivered *after* some brain cells were already damaged.

Another example of how important timing can be comes from a recent study completed by our university colleagues Drs. Dunkin and Rasgon (2006). They found that women who had recently become postmenopausal were more likely to benefit from ERT than those who had been postmenopausal for several years. This first category of women improved on what are called *executive functioning tasks* (ability to organize, be flexible, and plan ahead).

These recent discoveries indicate the potential importance of HRT during early menopause in particular. They also point to a connection between HRT and a decreased risk of Alzheimer's disease.

Dementia Scare

If women taking HRT have better verbal memory, this might explain why these women are less likely to develop dementia. When we are talking about *dementia*, we are usually talking about *Alzheimer's disease*, a disorder associated with severe memory impairment that is the most common type of dementia. Women are more likely than men to get dementia. This may be due to two factors. First, women are more likely to live longer than men, and the biggest risk factor for dementia is age, because as we age, the changes that naturally occur in our brain put us at greater risk for memory impairment. Second, estrogen deficiency in the hippocampus may put women at greater risk than men for dementia. Initially, this might not make sense, but men always have some level of estrogen available to their brain because testosterone converts to estrogen within the male brain.

Let's take a closer look at age and estrogen and their impact on memory impairment or dementia. Just how many people get dementia depends upon what age group you look at. For example, people younger than 65 are rarely diagnosed with dementia unless they have a genetic risk or some other medical cause for their memory impairment. Only about 5 to 8 percent of people ages sixty-five to eighty are likely to have dementia. This increases dramatically to 20 percent or more after age eighty. Within these groups, postmenopausal women are 1.4 to 3 times more likely to have dementia. This points to the estrogen-memory link that we have been talking about. With these kinds of numbers, it is possible to say that estrogen deficiency may be related to the dementia scare. Further evidence for this link comes from several research studies that conclude that postmenopausal women taking HRT are less likely to develop Alzheimer's disease. There have been more than a dozen well-established studies that report HRT users are 30 to 50 percent less likely to be at risk for dementia (Le Blanc et al. 2001; Greene and Dixon 2002).

If estrogen deficiency is related to worsening memory and possibly to the risk for dementia, can we actually see a difference in the brains of postmenopausal women—taking HRT and not? Brain scans or pictures of the brain help to answer this question.

Pictures of the Brain: Increased Metabolism

Why is there the possibility that HRT users are less depressed than those not using HRT? Why do HRT users have better memory function, and why are they less likely to get dementia when compared to those not using HRT? Let's talk about metabolism. When we think of *metabolism*, we typically think about the ability to burn calories and about weight gain and loss. There are actually different types of metabolism. Metabolism in the brain involves increased blood flow, and how it pertains to the ability to function, and function well. It is believed that if you have higher brain metabolism, your brain is probably working more, perhaps even better. This is important because decreases in brain metabolism are associated with a higher risk for dementia (Cohen, Andreason, and Sunderland 1997).

To get a better sense of this, let's turn to actually looking at interactive pictures of the brain in what we call *positron-emission tomography* or *PET imaging*. These PET images are not pictures of your dog or cat; they are snapshots of how your brain, specifically the metabolism of your brain, is working. It is only in the past few years that we have been able to detect differences between the brains of HRT users and non-HRT users. Seven or more studies have been published, including two of our studies from UCLA, that show that postmenopausal women using HRT have better brain metabolism than those not using HRT. The PET images show that the increase in metabolism has usually been found in the frontal and temporal regions of the brain (Resnick et al. 1998; Costa et al. 1999; Eberling et al. 2000). These are the areas of the brain that are associated with better memory, including being better able to encode and retrieve (recall) new information. The frontal region of the brain is also associated with better executive functioning, which we discussed earlier in the chapter with Drs. Dunkin and Rasgon's findings (2006) that recent postmenopausal women taking ERT improved on executive functioning tasks (ability to organize, be flexible, and plan ahead).

To be more specific, let's look at the studies we conducted at UCLA with Drs. Rasgon and Small. In our first study (Rasgon et al. 2001), we looked at a small sample of women who had been taking HRT (both unopposed and combination). The estrogen users (both the ERT and HRT users) had better metabolism in the temporal region of the brain than did the non-estrogen users. This finding is critical and interesting, because this area of the brain is often associated with better memory functioning. We also followed these same women over time. After a few years, the estrogen users had not experienced any decline in their brain metabolism, but the nonusers had (Rasgon et al. 2005). This is important as well, because it not only tells us that estrogen users have better brain metabolism, but also that they are less likely to show a decline over time. It is the decline over time that puts people at risk for a memory disorder like dementia. While our sample sizes were small, this research extends the research of others and points to a need for future research in a similar area. We need to better understand the direct impact of estrogen on the brain and the body, rather than just following women through time and examining symptoms and disease correlations after the fact.

Mood & Memory Connection

If you are wondering why we are spending all this time on the brain and memory—and just how they might be linked to depression—you are asking the right question. There is no complete answer yet, but many of us are wondering about the link. If estrogen deficiency is linked to depression and to memory problems, is there also an interaction between the two? We do know that people who are depressed don't perform as well as others on memory tasks. We also know that people who are depressed may also be at a greater risk for a memory disorder like dementia (Greerlings et al. 2000; Elderkin-Thompson et al. 2004; Dal Forno et al. 2005). Using MRI imaging, Dr. Kumar and colleagues (1998, 2000) from UCLA have observed *atrophy* (brain shrinking) in the frontal lobes of those who are depressed, which gets worse as the person becomes more depressed. These changes in the brain, including progressively more-impaired cognitive functioning, may not fully remit or get better, even with treatment (Alexopoulos et al. 2000; Butters et al. 2000).

The important thing to keep in mind is that estrogen deficiency seems to be linked not only to a host of physical symptoms, which we talked about in chapter 5 on menopause, but also to specific changes in the brain. These changes may put a woman at risk for depression and memory problems, including the possible risk for dementia.

Real-Life Connections

Just how significant can this impact on mood and memory really be? Is there really a connection between mood and memory in the daily lives of women? Let's meet Florence. She reported a lifelong battle with depression, a battle that got much worse with menopause. In fact, it became so bad that she initially had to go on disability because she could no longer function at work. It started off with crying jags; she would lock herself in the bathroom because her boss had snapped at her. But then she just started to avoid work altogether. She called in sick frequently and found herself thinking of any type of excuse to "work" from home and not go into the office. Even when working from home, she did not feel like her concentration or her memory were what they used to be. Her relationships also suffered. Already divorced and feeling a bit lonely, she felt even more cut off from a social life. She did not reach out and call friends but waited on the sidelines for her friends to call her. She was snippy and yet vague with her grown son when he called to check on her. She stopped going to her temple and rarely even stopped at the grocery store to buy food. After a while, she realized that she was barely existing. When she saw her friends and son around the holidays, they were shocked by her appearance and demeanor. Florence had lost her spark, and she seemed gaunt, tired, and worn out. They also noticed that she seemed distracted, unable to pay attention, and that she was more forgetful than before. After some prodding from her son, Florence sought medical help. Her physician felt her depression was due to a combination of menopause and life circumstances. He recommended a combination of ERT and an antidepressant. Within a few months Florence had regained her energy, felt her old spark, and was able to return to work with renewed confidence in her emotional and overall cognitive state.

Window of Opportunity

Given a link between estrogen and depression, and taking into account this new information about memory and dementia, is there a critical opportunity for protection? Most likely, yes. The more we learn about estrogen deficiency and its effect on the brain, including impact on mood and memory, the more we realize that it is probably optimal to treat the estrogen deficiency during perimenopause. The addition of HRT or ERT may offer the much-needed *neuroprotection* (protecting brain cells) and possibly *neuroenhancement* (increasing the ability and activity of the brain cells). What we do not know is how long you need to take some type of estrogen replacement (ERT or HRT) to remain optimally protected. Some women might only take estrogen replacement for a few years, while others might stay on it for decades. Do these two approaches yield differences in depression, memory, and protection of the brain? This question has yet to be answered by science. The government sponsored a study that had hoped to answer this question, but it was stopped prematurely for several reasons. Let's take a look at that study, including the scare of rising rates of cancer.

Misleading Information

The highly publicized discontinuation of the Women's Health Initiative (WHI), first in July 2002 and again in February 2004, resulted in a media frenzy of misleading information that has greatly impacted both the public and the medical community's view of HRT. In many ways this has been an unjust scare. To really understand the issues, we must first return to the original source, the WHI study itself, rather than the media's portrayal of the study (Rossouw et al. 2002; WHI 2004).

The WHI study proposed to study the effects of HRT, including both estrogen alone and estrogen with progesterone. The goal of the study was initially to understand the impact of HRT on menopause, particularly in terms of the prevention of coronary heart disease. But the study was stopped after only a few years because some women developed cancer and other medical complications. What the media did not clearly report was the actual number of women who developed cancer in both the treatment and nontreatment conditions of the study. These cancers developed in less than 1 to 2 percent of all the women in the study (out of more than ten thousand). The numbers were very small. For example, the number of women taking HRT (estrogen and progesterone) who developed breast cancer was thirty-eight (out of ten thousand)—this was compared to the thirty non-HRT users who developed breast cancer. This difference of eight women was touted as a 26 percent increased risk. Recent researchers have suggested that the design of the study and the exclusion of significant variables (age of menopause, reproductive risk factors, and so on) might actually account for the risk ratio of breast cancer rather than use of HRT (Garbe, Levesque, and Suissa 2004). To clarify further, a woman in this study may have already been at risk for cancer, whether or not she entered the study, based on family history or some other factor. Taking HRT in this study may not have been the direct cause of her cancer. Put another way, the media used some "fancy math" that does not accurately reflect the overall risk ratio of getting breast cancer.

Let's put these numbers in perspective. Let's say you and I wanted to raise $10,000 to send a friend on a cruise around the world and we sent out ten thousand letters to family, friends, and strangers, asking for a $1 donation. If you got thirty responses and raised $30, while I got thirty-eight responses and raised $38, I would technically be 26 percent more successful than you. But we would both have fallen very short of our goal to raise $10,000. In fact, together we would have raised less than 1 percent of our goal. The purpose of this story is to emphasize that numbers must be considered in the context of the bigger picture. In the case of HRT and breast cancer, 1 to 2 percent is a very low number, just as in our fundraising story, 1 to 2 percent of the $10,000 needed will not get our friend a dream cruise. We are best informed when we actually look at the original source for science and data rather than at an interpretation from the media.

Get the Facts on Breast Cancer

This raises the importance of getting the facts, including understanding what it is that we don't know. For example, keep in mind that we don't know just how at risk these women were for cancer prior to the study. Perhaps their genetics, family history, or previous lifestyle issues put them at greater risk for cancer. We do know that the women in the WHI study tended to be overweight, which may create a greater risk for cancer than use of HRT (Amy 2005; Kuhl 2005). The entire design and implementation of the WHI study has also been called into question (Machens and Schmidt-Gollwitzer 2003). Criticisms of the study include the age of the women selected to be studied, the biostatistics (how the numbers were crunched), the clinical endpoints (determining who developed cancer), and the dropout rate, which skews a sample because you are only studying a select group of women that decided to stay in the study.

Perhaps the most important of these criticisms for us to consider is the age of the women in the WHI study. Throughout this book, we have talked about the importance of thinking about menopausal stages, and now in this chapter we have talked about the timing of treatment for symptoms. In the WHI study, the women had been postmenopausal for at least ten years. The critical window for treating menopause and starting HRT was long past. This means that we cannot generalize from the WHI study to younger women, who are perimenopausal or recently postmenopausal. At best, even if we buy into the media scare regarding the WHI results, we can say that HRT is not for women over sixty-five years old, and even that is a gross generalization that may not be accurate. Not only is it impossible to make generalizations from the WHI study, but their results are also not consistent with forty years of other research studies. Dr. Nelson and colleagues (2002) set out to look at this cancer scare by looking at breast cancer research studies from the past forty years, including a reanalysis of the data from the WHI study. Their results indicated that the increase for cancer with the use of HRT was minimal to none. And there was no increased risk for breast cancer with a past history of using HRT. It gets further complicated because it appears that the overall death rate from breast cancer is actually slightly reduced in women with a prior history of using HRT (Vassilopoulou-Sellin 2003). To summarize briefly, if you are taking HRT, you might be at greater risk, in the moment, for breast cancer, because we know that estrogen can accelerate the growth of cancer cells. But having used HRT at some time in your life does not increase your overall risk for breast cancer, and having used HRT might actually lower your chances of dying from breast cancer (possibly because of early detection when using HRT). Once again, timing is everything.

Estrogen, Depression & Health

Understanding the possible link between estrogen and the treatment of depression in women is not only critical for improved mood, but also for overall health. For example, the WHI study suggested that depression in postmenopausal women increases their risk of cardiovascular disease (Wassertheil-Smoller et al. 2004). Just as we discussed with perimenopause, the complex link between physical state and emotional well-being makes it increasingly important to consider the role of estrogen in the *etiology* (cause) and treatment of postmenopausal depression.

Have Heart

Understanding the impact of estrogen deficiency and treatment on the heart in postmenopausal women is critical. Women are more likely to die from coronary heart disease than any other medical complication. Risk of death from heart disease may be as high as 31 percent, whereas breast cancer may be as low as 3 percent (Cummings, Black, and Rubin 1989). Just as the breast cancer issue is debated, so is HRT and its impact on cardiovascular (heart) health. Based on the results of over thirty years of research and three dozen studies, it was thought that estrogen benefited the heart, including a 50 percent decreased risk of death from heart disease (Judd 1996). The WHI study changed that school of thought, with the latest understanding that there may be no difference in risk between HRT users and nonusers (Bromley et al. 2005). But now the results of the WHI study are being questioned. Post-WHI research is showing once again that use of estrogen may lower risk for cardiovascular events by 34 percent (Rossano et al. 2003). Perhaps we are back to square one. Most likely estrogen is not the causative factor for heart problems, but rather personal medical history and genetics, with estrogen as a mediating or contributing factor, depending on the timing of use.

Do Not Be Misled

The bottom line is that we have to get the facts from the direct sources, and from the leading experts, by actually reading the original research documents that are produced by the researchers and published within a peer-reviewed process for the medical community. The newscasters, magazine journalists, and even our personal physicians may not understand the complexity of estrogen research. This hotly debated subject is more complex than "just saying no" to HRT. There's an intricate balance between neuroscience, estrogen's impact on the brain, and a woman's personal medical history.

To drive the point home, we want to share some personal thoughts that were once imparted to us by a very well-respected researcher. Just as we were being exposed to the world of the brain, mood functioning, and hormones, this scientist talked about her own personal choice between HRT and the risk of breast cancer. Without a prompt from us, she made a dramatic yet simple statement: "I will take my brain over my breasts, any day." This powerful statement fueled our interest to know more, to understand just how important estrogen is to the functioning of the brain. Hers may not be the sentiment of every woman, and we recognize that for some women the threat of breast cancer, because of family history or genetic basis, is the most central aspect of the choice to not use HRT. Nevertheless, such a powerful statement from a scientist encouraged us to continue to pursue an understanding of how estrogen impacts the brain and mood functioning, despite the possible risk for cancer.

Additional Benefits of HRT

Thus far we have focused on better mood, improved brain functioning (memory), and understanding the cancer scare. What about that long list of menopause symptoms that we first addressed in chapter 5? How does HRT impact those symptoms? We know that the domino theory suggests a connection between these symptoms and mood (that is, that experiencing these physical symptoms may contribute to a woman's depression). We need to look at how HRT might improve some of these other menopausal symptoms.

We know that HRT and ERT users have better bone density than nonusers, putting them at lower risk for osteoporosis and hip fractures. Just how serious is a broken hip? Well, the numbers say that about 20 percent of those who break a hip due to osteoporosis will die within a year, another 20 percent do not walk again, and 50 percent will never walk as well as they did before the break (Cooper 1997). That leaves only about 10 percent virtually unaffected by a broken hip. These same estrogen users are also less likely to lose their teeth. The impact of estrogen replacement on bones and teeth is serious.

Perhaps less serious, but certainly annoying, if not distressing to the point of increasing depression, is the sleep disturbance that menopausal women experience. As many as 70 percent of women report better sleep with HRT. This impact is secondary to the already well-documented alleviation of symptoms like hot flashes, vaginal dryness, dry skin (increased collagen), muscle and joint aches, and so on (EMEA 2003). Estrogen users have fewer migraine headaches, less incontinence, and fewer urinary tract infections. They report improvement in sexual functioning, including arousal, sexual desire, and enjoyment (Alexander et al. 2004). Women taking HRT also tend to have lower cholesterol, a decreased risk for colorectal cancer, and are better able to manage their diabetes. Finally, HRT may also help with vision-related diseases like glaucoma and macular degeneration (Klein et al. 1994; Vingerling et al. 1995).

The impact of estrogen replacement (HRT or ERT) is pervasive. Not only does it improve mood and memory, but it helps the body system-wide. With the backlash from the WHI study, it has been reported by doctors and the media that millions of women have stopped taking HRT, but a few months or years later, these women felt their quality of life suffer and began rethinking the choice for HRT. When considering HRT, a woman and her physician must consider the whole picture, including the evolving scientific information on the benefits and risks of HRT. Understanding the overall impact of HRT is important so that women can make personal, individual, and informed decisions.

Conclusion

Menopause and its symptoms, including depression, are not just a state of mind. It is a phase of life that ushers in dramatic physical and mental changes. This chapter has focused on how hormone replacement therapy impacts the life of peri- and postmenopausal woman. There is a fairly clear understanding that HRT can improve the mood of women, both those with depression and those without. Most of our current understanding about mood functioning in menopausal women comes from the numerous research studies on HRT, which we explored in this chapter. We know that at least 50 percent or more of women report feeling better, that is, less depressed, with HRT. The impact on mood seems to extend beyond the improvement of just menopausal symptoms. It appears to be linked to a direct impact on the brain, affecting not only mood, but also memory and attention functions.

Mood and memory aside, HRT also seems to alleviate physical symptoms for most women. For example, with fewer hot flashes and improved sleep, women feel as if they have a better quality of everyday life. We also know that HRT may be helpful with serious medical issues, such as osteoporosis and colorectal cancer. What is not well understood is the timing of estrogen use. Do menopausal women need to use HRT for only a short duration, such as the window when symptoms occur and when the decline of estrogen takes a toll on the brain? Or should women use HRT for longer periods, if their medical history allows it? Science has yet to answer these questions.

Approximately forty million American women are currently facing menopause, yet only 25 percent of women elect to take traditional HRT treatment. This suggests two things. First, more women should be in dialogue with a menopause specialist, who clearly understands the benefits of HRT, to see if it is the right choice. Second, if traditional HRT is not the right choice, then alternative approaches should be considered and investigated. We will begin the exploration of alternative approaches in the next chapter.

CHAPTER 8

Alternative Approaches to Hormone Replacement Therapy

Ellen, a close friend of ours, wasn't interested in the traditional approaches to treating the symptoms of menopause. Sure, she was acutely suffering, but she had a very strong will. She did not want to go along with traditional Western medicine for this issue. This was unexpected because she worked in the medical field, and she certainly believed in antidepressants and a host of other medical treatments for her clients. Maybe it was the influence of her mother who was old world, old school, and had never taken anything to treat her own menopausal symptoms. Maybe it was the fact that Ellen was a feisty intellectual who liked the idea that her mind could control her body. Her resistance might even have been a reaction to an unexpressed fear of breast cancer. Whatever the reason, Ellen felt that the most personally appropriate choice for treating menopause was to take the alternative route. She consulted a person that she jokingly called the "witch doctor"—a menopause specialist who was armed with the latest information about treating menopause naturally. For Ellen, the recommended regimen included black cohosh, cream made from wild yam, changes in her lifestyle (more exercise, better nutrition, less alcohol), and participation in psychotherapy. Before we examine how this combination worked for Ellen, let's view some of these alternative treatment choices for menopause.

Alternative Choices

When we talk about alternative treatment choices, we are including a host of things from bio-identical estrogens and designer estrogens (SERMs) to herbal supplements and acupuncture to lifestyle changes and mind-altering approaches (like stress reduction and psychotherapy). While this chapter can hardly be a complete list of every option available, we will try to give you a good overview of the choices that are out there to help you make the best personal choice. Many of the choices we will describe are aimed at mood improvement and address the estrogen-depression connection; however, since there are so many symptoms related to menopause, in particular, we are also going to discuss alternative treatments for symptoms such as hot flashes or low sex drive. Remember the domino theory from chapter 5? If physical symptoms can affect our mood, then we also want to explore alternative treatments for them.

"The Sexy Years"

Bio-identical hormones have been around for years, but Suzanne Somers' book *The Sexy Years* (2004) has put them on the map. Bio-identical hormones have a molecular structure that is similar to your own body's hormones, but they come from plants. Examples of bio-identical hormones include, but are not limited to, *progest gel* (progesterone from wild yam and soy) and *triest gel* or *biest gel* (both are estrogen from wild yam and soy). Other commercially available products include the bio-identical progesterone Prometrium, and the bio-identical estradiols, like Estrace and generic preparations, along with the Climara and Femara patches. These products can be very helpful for women with estrogen deficiency and may be covered under an insurance plan. The drawback is that they only come in certain doses, and while a woman can double up or cut the dose in half, they are not customized to her as an individual. If your insurance covers it, or it feels affordable to you, you might want to consider personalized bio-identical hormones.

Get Personal

Bio-identical hormone replacements can be a specifically tailored option. A menopausal specialist (some pharmacists, for example) can cook up a combination that is personalized for you. First, a woman will have to have her hormone levels tested in order to determine an ideal balance. Not all physicians are experts in this area, so a woman needs to ask her doctor about expertise and background. A referral to a menopause specialist may be necessary. After examining the hormone levels, a prescription for a personalized compound of bio-identical HRT will be created.

To get a personalized compound, you need to have the prescription filled at a *compounding pharmacy*. This is generally not a chain store but an independently owned and operated pharmacy that can mix up the personalized combination. If you have a hard time locating a compounding pharmacy, try locating a nearby fertility treatment center or pain management center as these are prime markets for other compounds that will be made at these specialized pharmacies.

To best understand exactly how personal combinations of bio-identical hormones are made for the individual, we consulted our friend and colleague Dr. Raenel Matthews, who is a pharmacist and menopause educator in Arizona. She told us that the most common ingredients are many of those we mentioned earlier in the book, namely biest (80 percent estriol, 20 percent estradiol), triest (80 percent estriol, 10 percent estradiol, 10 percent estrone), progesterone, and testosterone. They come in pure powder form, and these molecules are identical biologically to what is (or used to be) produced in the human body. DHEA, as mentioned in chapter 6, is also available in this form. The source for these powders is usually soybeans. The plant "hormones" are isolated and then subjected to different chemical reactions that ultimately lead to the formation of progesterone. But once in this new form, our bodies are able to utilize the estrogen and progesterone from the bio-identical hormones. Dr. Matthews explains that with compounded formulations, doses can be designed for specific women because they are made in small batches right at the local pharmacy.

Natural Creams

Creams containing natural progesterone and/or *phytoestrogens* (estrogen-like elements found in plants) are available from a wide variety of companies. All you have to do is go online and you will see advertisements for hundreds of products, many of which are essentially the same. When you see names like "Natural Progesterone Cream" and "Estro-All Cream," you know you have hit the right links. If traditional HRT is not the right choice for you, one of these plant-based creams may be the optimal choice. They are often made of wild yam, soy, dong quai, black cohosh, or red clover. We will talk about these herbs more extensively later in this chapter, including the symptoms that they usually target, but let's first talk about the impact of bio-identical hormones.

IMPACT

Bio-identical hormones are thought to treat or reduce menopause symptoms, including hot flashes, night sweats, weight gain, insomnia, and lack of energy. They are also thought to improve self-perception of memory abilities, skin, and hair and to increase libido. We do not yet know if bio-identical hormones impact mood directly. Phytoestrogens' impact on the brain is currently being studied. Initial results in the lab show some protection for the neurons (brain cells), but the sustained impact or benefit is not well documented (Zhao, O'Neill, and Brinton 2005). Without sustained benefit, the improvement of memory or protection against dementia is not likely (Zhao, O'Neill, and Brinton 2005). Along the same lines, although soy has been used successfully to treat menopausal symptoms, it does not appear to be protective of the brain. For example, soy does not seem to improve memory in postmenopausal women (Rice, Graves, and Larson 1995; Kreijkamp-Kaspers et al. 2004). Therefore, the physical and emotional symptoms of menopause appear to be reduced by bio-identical hormones, but the impact of these phytoestrogens on the brain is less evident.

Being Selective

We talked earlier about the option of using SERMs (selective estrogen receptor modulators; see chapter 6 for a list). This alternative choice for estrogen replacement is a hot topic. The two most common SERMs are tamoxifen

(Nolvadex), which is used with breast cancer patients, and raloxifene (Evista), which is typically used in noncancer menopausal women to increase bone density. These are the only readily available SERMs. However, there are numerous others in the research and development phase, some of which we listed in chapter 6, so watch for them to be available in the very near future.

IMPACT

SERMs' ability to alleviate traditional symptoms of menopause is not well documented but is being studied in animal models (Wallace et al. 2006). In breast cancer patients, the use of tamoxifen may actually increase some symptoms like hot flashes. Its purpose is to actually block estrogen effects and decrease the chance for reoccurrence of breast cancer. Tamoxifen also does not appear to be beneficial for the brain (Paganini-Hill and Clark 2000), as women who remain on this SERM for more than five years perform worse on cognitive tests (for instance, for memory or attention span) when compared to women who use it for a shorter time. Work in the lab (using cells in a dish) shows that tamoxifen may promote neuron growth but not in the way that would result in better memory (Zhao, O'Neill, and Brinton 2005).

As with tamoxifen, raloxifene is not known as a treatment for hot flashes (Cranney and Adachi 2005), but it does appear to benefit menopausal women in other ways. First, it was designed to increase bone density, and research notes its success. Women taking raloxifene have an increase of 2.5 percent bone density in their spine within the first few years, are 30 to 50 percent less likely to have vertebral fractures, and have a 72 percent decrease in risk for breast cancer (Cranney and Adachi 2005). Raloxifene also has a positive impact on lipids and fat distribution (Francucci et al. 2005). This may be important because, as we mentioned in chapter 7, an increase in body mass index (BMI) may be the greatest risk for health concerns like cancer.

The impact of raloxifene on the brain is currently being studied. Initially, Dr. Yaffe and colleagues (2001) found no effect of raloxifene on the cognitive scores for postmenopausal women during a three-year time period. When Dr. Yaffe and colleagues reexamined the data for these same women, they noticed that the specific dose of raloxifene had an impact on cognitive ability. Namely, those women taking 120 milligrams per day differed from those taking 60 milligrams or not taking any raloxifene (instead taking a placebo or sugar pill). The women taking the higher dose had a 33 percent lower risk for mild cognitive impairment (Yaffe et al. 2005). These are important results because *mild cognitive impairment* (MCI) is believed to be a precursor to dementia. Recently, within the lab setting where neurons (brain cells) are studied, there has been some hopeful news that low doses would be beneficial, but the neuroprotection against dementia remains unclear (Zhao, O'Neill, and Brinton 2005). When considering Dr. Zhao's results in relation to Dr. Yaffe's results, it is clear that we need more information on what the ideal dose for protection of the brain would be.

Just as we need additional information on raloxifene's impact on the brain and cognition, we also need more information on its possible augmentation for treatment of depression. One very small study has been completed with strong results that show raloxifene taken with an antidepressant can help to alleviate *treatment-resistant depression*, that is, depression that does not respond to traditional medical approaches (McIntyre and Fulton 2005).

Au Naturel

There are various natural supplements available that have historically been used to treat symptoms associated with PMS, postpartum depression, and menopause. These include, but are not limited to, herbs and creams from natural derivatives of estrogen and progesterone as well as homeopathic remedies.

Before using any of the alternative treatments it is particularly important that you address your symptoms and current health situation with your physician. Many of these alternative choices may not be right for you, and in some cases may be dangerous, particularly if you are breastfeeding or taking other prescription medications. You should use the information in this chapter as a guide for what options you might explore, with the approval of your physician.

HERBS

There are numerous herbs with phytoestrogens (estrogen-like elements found in plants). There are also herbs that influence the metabolism of estrogen. The estrogenic action of these phytoestrogen compounds is significantly less than it is for native human estradiol, ranging from a hundredth to a thousandth of the potency. Finally, there are additional herbs that we will discuss that do not have estrogen-like elements nor do they influence the metabolism of estrogen, but they are known to have some impact on menopausal or PMS symptoms.

Be aware that there are two main families of herbs—isoflavone and lignan—that can be found on some of the labels of the herbal supplements you may purchase. First, let's take a look at these two families of herbs, and then let's look at the specific herbs that are associated with relief for certain symptoms.

FAMILIES OF HERBS

Isoflavone Family	Lignan Family
Biochanin A	Enterodiol
Coumestrol	Enterolactone
Daidzein	Matairesinol
Daidzin	Secoisolariciresinol
Equol	
Formononetin	
Genistein	
Prunetin	

Isoflavones are compounds produced mainly from *Leguminosae* (bean family) and are known for their estrogen-like effects on mammals. They are considered strong antioxidants and have a history of use for lowering cholesterol, protecting against cancer, and enhancing fertility. An example of an isoflavone source is the soybean, which contains the isoflavones genistein and daidzein (listed above). *Lignans* are fiber-related compounds that influence estrogen and testosterone metabolism. An example of a lignan is flaxseed, which is considered rich in omega (3, 6, and 9) fatty acids and helpful in maintaining a healthy immune system. Flaxseed is also being studied as an inhibitor for the growth and development of cancer. Here is a list of herbs that are often used to treat menopause symptoms. Let's take a look at the list and the symptoms they are known to address:

HERBS OF INTEREST FOR MENOPAUSE SYMPTOMS

Black cohosh (Remifemin)

Black currant

Chamomile

Chasteberry

Cooling herbs (chickweed, elder flower, and violet)

Dong quai

Echinacea

Evening primrose

Flaxseed oil

Garlic

Ginkgo biloba

Ginseng

Green tea

Kava

Red clover (Promensil)

Saint-John's-wort

Valerian root

Wild yam

GINSENG, DONG QUAI, BLACK COHOSH, RED CLOVER, CHASTEBERRY: HOT FLASHES & MORE

Ginseng, dong quai, black cohosh (also called squaw root, black snake root, or rattle weed), red clover, and chasteberry are thought to have *estrogenic potency*, or an estrogen-like impact, although that impact is much less than what is available from HRT. Two of these natural sources are now standardized and marketed as Remifemin (black cohosh) and Promensil (red clover). Often they will be used in some combination to treat menstrual disorders or symptoms of menopause, including depression, low sex drive, insomnia, hot flashes, and fatigue.

CAUTION! *There can be complications with the use of these herbs, including heavy menstrual periods, fibroids, blood thinning, or diarrhea, so caution should be applied in their use, which should be monitored closely (Huston and Lanka 2001). Remember to consult your physician before beginning any type of alternative treatment as it may have interactions with other medications.*

WILD YAM: CRAMPS & MORE

Wild yam contains a progesterone precursor that is used by the pharmaceutical industry. Extracts and creams made from wild yam (and often other herbs) are promoted as treatment for cramps and for relaxing muscles, soothing nerves, and pain relief. During pregnancy, wild yam is sometimes used to prevent miscarriage or alleviate nausea. Suppliers also claim it is useful for nervousness and restlessness.

FLAXSEED OIL, BLACK CURRANT, EVENING PRIMROSE: PMS

Both flaxseed oil and black currant oil are good sources of omega fatty acids and are thought to help with PMS symptoms, including breast tenderness. Evening primrose is a good source of omega-6 fatty acid, specifically, and also helps with PMS symptoms.

CHICKWEED, ELDER FLOWER, VIOLET: HOT FLASHES

Whether alone or in combination, chickweed, elder flower, and violet are considered *cooling herbs* that can lower the body's thermostat to address hot flashes.

SAINT-JOHN'S-WORT: MOOD IMPROVEMENT

Saint-John's-wort is touted as "nature's Prozac" because it is thought to have antidepressant-like qualities, including ten compounds that have drug-like effects. Saint-John's-wort is not only used by postmenopausal women; women suffering from depression related to PMS or postpartum depression might also seek out "nature's Prozac."

CAUTION! *Because of its potential potency, caution should be applied when using Saint-John's-wort with other medications, and you should consult your physician before using it. This caution is particularly important if you are breastfeeding, in which case you certainly want to consult your physician before trying Saint-John's-wort or any other natural remedy.*

VALERIAN ROOT, KAVA, CHAMOMILE: RELAXATION & SLEEP

Valerian root has mild sedative effects that promote better sleep. Kava (also known as *kava kava* or *kawa*) is used as a remedy for insomnia and anxiety. Chamomile is a well-known herb used as a tea to promote sleeping and reduce cramps.

GINKGO BILOBA: MEMORY

Often referred to just as *ginkgo*, this herb is known for its antioxidant properties, which are thought to help protect the brain from damage by free radicals (as with estrogen, as mentioned in chapter 1, it potentially clears out the toxins). This herb is thought to improve concentration and memory. If purchasing this herb, be sure it includes the only known standardized extract: EGb761.

GARLIC, ECHINACEA, GREEN TEA: IMMUNE SYSTEM

Used to lower cholesterol and blood pressure, garlic is being studied for cancer prevention and enhancement of the immune system. Echinacea is used to boost the immune system, particularly from winter infections. Green tea has antioxidant properties that may lower the risk of cancer and promote a better immune system.

IMPACT

The ability of these herbal supplements to actually improve menopause symptoms is controversial, with very few studies offering well-documented success. A recent publication reviewed the benefits of black cohosh, including treatment for hot flashes, sweating, anxiety, and insomnia. But they also warned that side effects may include headaches, dizziness, nausea, and weight gain, to name just a few (Mahady 2005).

Given the lack of available data, a patient's self-report of improvement is often the only measure of success. Future research will need to focus on improving our understanding of their impact as compared to that of traditional treatment approaches or a placebo. There is no available data regarding the impact of herbal treatments on cardiovascular disease or osteoporosis. Many of these herbs have little or no estrogen, so there is no evidence to date that they will improve memory as with traditional treatment. The exception to this includes some limited research on the positive effects of ginkgo on memory (Mix and Crews 2002; Wesnes et al. 2000); however, not all research studies have found a positive effect (van Dongen et al. 2000). Currently there is a longitudinal study under way to examine the benefits of ginkgo on memory, but it will be approximately five years before we know the results (DeKosky et al. 2006). The global and specific impact of herbs on menopause and menopausal symptoms are areas of much-needed future research. Furthermore, very few have investigated how herbs and other natural remedies might be useful and helpful to treat depression and other symptoms related to estrogen imbalance, such as PMS and postpartum depression.

CAUTION!

It is important to apply caution when considering herbal treatments because there is no Food and Drug Administration (FDA) approval for these remedies. Without standardization, it is difficult to be sure of the active ingredients (single or multiple botanicals), and the dosing may be different for each brand or even each *lot* (doses grouped at the time of manufacturing).

As mentioned above, another reason to be cautious is that some herbs, such as ginseng, dong quai, black cohosh, red clover, and chasteberry, may cause heavy menstrual periods, fibroids, blood thinning, or diarrhea; therefore, their use should be monitored closely (Huston and Lanka 2001).

We hope that you find the descriptions of the natural supplements helpful, but we do want to caution you that no one should make a self-diagnosis and then create a self-prescribed treatment. Just because these remedies are readily available to you at your local health food store doesn't mean that they are going to necessarily be the right choice for you or be helpful. In fact, sometimes they can be harmful if used incorrectly or in conjunction with each other or other medications. It is also important to be cautious with any medications or remedies when you are breastfeeding.

Always consult your physician and pharmacist to discuss your medical history, current symptoms, personal needs, and treatment choices. This is critical because natural remedies can have interactions with other prescriptions and over-the-counter medications.

Checking on Ellen

We are going to talk about some of the additional routes taken by Ellen, the woman we introduced at the beginning of this chapter. But first, let's see what Ellen thought about her doctor's suggestion of black cohosh and a cream made from wild yam. Initially, Ellen reported that she felt no relief from this combination. She was particularly bothered by her low sex drive and the hot flashes that were increasing both in frequency and intensity. The natural menopause specialist told her to increase the doses. Ellen then felt a difference, especially a reduction in hot flashes, but then she started having some side effects. Because Ellen was in perimenopause, she was still occasionally having menstrual periods, but now they were much heavier and felt more painful. After consulting with the specialist, Ellen understood that the standard dose of Remifemin (marketed label for black cohosh) was too strong for her, particularly because she is very petite and weighs only one hundred pounds. The menopause specialist helped her to find a combination of black cohosh and dong quai that was tolerable yet still gave her relief from the hot flashes. The specialist also explained to Ellen that if this combination did not have a successful impact, she might want to try a personalized bio-identical hormone compound. Keeping this next step in mind, the specialist then encouraged Ellen to follow up with the other suggestions, including lifestyle changes and psychotherapy. Let's take a look at how these treatments can impact the estrogen-depression connection for women.

More of Eastern Medicine

Natural supplements are considered a cornerstone of Eastern medicine. Most experts in Eastern medicine spend years studying these supplements and their impact on health, including mood functioning. We now turn to some additional aspects of Eastern medicine that might be useful in treating depression for women, no matter what age.

Homeopathy

The basic concept of homeopathy is that "like will be cured by like," or in other words, whatever is causing the problem can also cure the problem. Very small doses of substances that cause symptoms are given to the person to address the condition. The belief behind homeopathy is that the small dose will invoke a response—your body will create a defense against the already present symptoms. In other words, the body will strengthen and heal itself. This is similar to what happens when we receive inoculation shots: we are given small portions of the various illnesses themselves so that the immune system builds up a defense against them.

Homeopathy can be controversial, and while we don't have time to explain it with depth in this book, it is something that some people turn to when addressing the estrogen-depression connection. Drs. Huston and Lanka (2001) in their book on perimenopause give an introduction to homeopathy. Within this presentation, they mention several possible homeopathic remedies for menopause. Often citing a book by Ullman (1991), these authors mention that sepia (inky secretion from cuttlefish), evening primrose (weed), lachesis (venom from bushmaster snake), pulsatilla (windflower), nux vomica (poisonous nut), and bioflavonoids (soy, spices, green tea, citrus fruits) are all available to treat symptoms of menopause, particularly hot flashes, low sex drive, sleep disturbances, and irritability/sadness.

IMPACT

Very little is known about the actual impact of these homeopathic remedies on symptom reduction and health protection. More research on all types of botanical (plant) therapies is needed, including research studies that are conducted with a placebo (no treatment) and standardization of the doses.

Acupuncture
Acupuncture is the practice of inserting tiny needles into specific locations of the body for therapeutic results. Typically considered safe, acupuncture can be harmful if performed incorrectly.

IMPACT
Because of the variability of studies, reliable data on acupuncture is hard to come by, but it is touted as successful for alleviating menopausal symptoms like hot flashes and headaches (Wyon et al. 1995; Vincent 1989). Recently the impact of acupuncture on hot flashes was documented in a research study. The results indicated relief after only twelve weeks of treatment and showed that this relief was sustained even six months after the treatment was completed (Nedstrand et al. 2005a).

Lifestyle Changes

Adding herbal supplements into your life, not to mention undertaking acupuncture, are lifestyle changes that many embrace. There are additional lifestyle changes that we need to address, namely, diet and exercise. Both of these can be crucial to addressing estrogen-related mood changes throughout a woman's life span.

Diet
Are you eating healthfully? A nutritionist can help design a diet that is personalized and addresses what you need, especially as a new mother or as a peri- or postmenopausal woman. We all know that a diet rich in fruits and vegetables is important as it provides antioxidants. If possible, try to eat whole foods rather than processed foods to get more nutrients. It is also important to make sure you drink enough water. Usually eight glasses of eight ounces or more is the recommended daily amount. In addition to the right foods

and an abundance of water, it is important to take vitamins. In particular, we know that for some women, vitamin E can reduce hot flashes and may improve memory. Calcium and vitamin D are important for bone density, but it is critical to know that these two supplements alone can slow, but not prevent, the bone loss that is associated with estrogen deficiency (Castelo-Branco et al. 2005). There is also some evidence that magnesium may improve estrogen's protective effect on the central nervous system, including enhanced cerebral blood flow, which may result in clearer thinking (Seelig, Altura, and Altura 2004).

Food choices can also have an impact. Hot and spicy foods, caffeine, and alcohol can trigger hot flashes while soy can be beneficial. We currently know that soy has estrogen-modulating effects; in other words, it helps to balance female hormones. As we learned in chapter 1, a balance of hormones (in particular, estrogen) is central to numerous aspects that may affect mood. In addition, soy also lowers cholesterol, has anticancer effects, and is believed to be an antioxidant.

Exercise

Daily exercise is important at any age but particularly so for women who might be feeling depressed. Exercise can actually be a natural antidepressant. As we get the heart rate going, we produce endorphins, which elevate our mood via brain chemistry. You don't have to be a marathon runner or an avid exerciser, but if you are—good for you! Even a daily, brisk walk for twenty minutes or more can help. Others prefer swimming or sports like tennis. The choice is yours, but the key is to get out and do it.

It is never too late to start exercising. A recent study, out this year, found that menopausal women who participated in a year-long exercise program reported better mental and physical health, while those who did not exercise actually felt worse than when they entered the study, possibly due to the impact of menopause and it symptoms (Villaverde-Gutierrez et al. 2006).

MAKING SMART CHOICES

When you decide to address both diet and exercise in your life, you are thinking about smart choices that impact your overall well-being. The impact of these choices can help to mediate some of the changes in mood that you might feel during an estrogen-related mood-sensitive time period, such as PMS, postpartum depression, or menopause. We know that women who eat a sensible diet and include exercise in their daily or weekly routine are more likely to have a lower *body mass index* (BMI). As we discussed in chapter 5, your BMI is your weight in ratio to your height. When your BMI exceeds 30, you are considered obese or severely overweight. People with lower BMIs are at less risk for many diseases, including cardiovascular (heart) disease, diabetes, high blood pressure, failure of the pancreas, and liver disease, just to name a few (Wood et al. 2006; DeWaele et al. 2006; Geiss et al. 2006; Crane, Van Rompaey, and Kitahata 2006; Jaskiewicz et al. 2006). Despite the link between BMI and health problems, the risk of death due to obesity is hotly debated and there are no firm conclusions (Janssen, Katzmarzyk, and Ross 2005). To check out your own BMI, go to the Internet where you will find a number of calculators that will compute your BMI for you in a matter of seconds (for example, see http://health.msn.com/dietfitness/bmicalculator.aspx). Consider how your own BMI might put you at risk for health problems and what choices you might make regarding diet and exercise to lower your BMI.

Other smart choices are as simple as stopping smoking. We know that smoking is linked to hot flashes and puts you at risk for many serious diseases, such as strokes, cancer, and heart attacks. Also something as simple as keeping cool can help you with menopausal symptoms. Wear layers of clothing, keep the air flowing in the room, and drink cold beverages to relieve hot flashes. Most would agree that if you are able to get cool and comfortable, it can lift your mood.

IMPACT

Hundreds of research studies show the importance of improved diet and exercise on overall well-being. Better health is often a matter of feeling better physically and mentally. It is important to take care of your body as well as your mind. If you want a simple approach to improving your diet, exercise, and mind, try reading Dr. Gary Small's *The Memory Prescription* (Small and Vorgan 2004). The book will give you tips on how to eat better, exercise more, reduce your stress, and improve your memory. We have seen firsthand when women try Dr. Small's approach the impact it has on their overall well-being. The desired effect is to feel better about yourself, so let's take a look at other options for altering your emotional state.

Mind-Altering Approaches

When we talk about "mind altering," we are not talking about some drug-induced trip; rather we are talking about how to alter your thinking or approach to situations, symptoms, relationships, and such. By changing your approach, you can begin to feel better. This is particularly important to the estrogen-depression connection because it gives you the opportunity to control some of the outcome that may be related to this internal biochemical process. Let's take a look at what we mean.

Stress Reduction

Stress reduction might be achieved through formal means, such as therapy (discussed below), or it might be achieved through things like relaxation. Meditation, relaxation exercises, biofeedback, or yoga are examples of how to lower your stress and improve your mood. Stress reduction also comes in the form of better social support. When we have close friends or family to talk to about our problems, we feel less stressed. Hypnosis is also used at times to reduce levels of stress. If you think one or more of these approaches would be of interest to you, we suggest that you look into finding a book or an expert to guide you in implementing approaches to lessen the stress in your life.

IMPACT

To date there are no research studies on how stress reduction impacts a woman's menopause symptoms, but stress reduction can improve overall mood. While it may not be the be-all and end-all for every physical or mental symptom that you are experiencing because of the estrogen-depression connection, these helpful techniques might give you back some control over your reactions to your symptoms.

Psychotherapy

Seeking help from a professional therapist, such as a psychologist, psychiatrist, marriage and family therapist, or social worker, can be a very successful approach to treating depression and other mood symptoms associated with estrogen deficiency, such as postpartum or menopausal depression. There are several types of therapy available, including, but not limited to, cognitive behavioral, interpersonal, and psychodynamic therapy. Let's take a look at a few of these to see which type might be right for you.

COGNITIVE BEHAVIORAL THERAPY

Also known as CBT, *cognitive behavioral therapy* focuses on changing faulty thinking (cognitions) and the way in which they impact your behavior. CBT therapists usually consider themselves collaborative and active in their approach to depression, with a focus on immediate goals and reduction of symptoms. The cognitive part of the therapy focuses on changing your thinking patterns to reduce depressive thoughts. You will be able to challenge your thoughts by first trying to predict the outcome and then actually documenting the outcome and realizing that things usually work out much better than you've imagined they will. This involves realizing that your memory may be selective and that you might only be remembering the negative things rather than tallying up the positive things that have happened as well. By becoming skeptical of your thoughts, especially in moments when you feel overly emotional, you stop taking your feelings at face value and try to prevent yourself from becoming emotionally flooded in the moment.

The behavioral aspect of CBT targets a change in your behavioral reactions to these same situations, where your thinking is faulty. The focus is on calming your body and mind so that you can think more clearly, make better decisions, and feel better, rather than reacting with self-damaging actions. This might be achieved in a variety of ways, such as repetitively facing this type of situation head-on until it feels less disturbing, or recognizing the differences between your thoughts, emotions, and bodily sensations. The CBT therapist would work on these and other approaches with you.

CBT focuses on changing thoughts, feelings, or behaviors, resulting in a change in the entire person. Reducing negative self-talk and replacing it with more positive self-perceptions or optimistic thinking will translate into new feelings and behaviors. In a similar fashion, the adoption of more positive behaviors and actions will result in more positive thoughts and feelings because it is difficult to act one way and think another. Let's look at an example of how CBT might work.

Jill never really struggled with depression until menopause hit. At the same time menopause snuck up on her, she also switched departments at her job and had to face several strangers on a daily basis. Now she felt constantly depressed and told herself that she was worthless and could not do anything right. When her office mates said hello in the morning, she mumbled her response. She rarely smiled when her boss complimented her work and often cried at the littlest critique or request to do something different. Finally, she refused to join her office mates at the coffee break but remained at her desk, keeping her sullen thoughts to herself. The CBT therapist helped Jill focus her negative thoughts. As they worked together actively, both realized that Jill only heard the criticisms from her boss but never took into account the praise she received. After a few weeks of challenging her negative thoughts, Jill began to have a more balanced view of what kind of feedback her boss was actually giving her. Her doctor also encouraged her to say hello or good morning to her coworkers when they greeted her. Finally, they were working toward the goal of having Jill join her coworkers at the coffee break and maybe even ask one of them out to lunch. In a few short weeks, Jill was beginning to see a difference in her overall outlook toward life.

INTERPERSONAL THERAPY

Also known as IPT, *interpersonal therapy* focuses on relationships and their impact on your life. IPT therapists tend to start with the present-day relationships, whether that involves the loss or lack of a relationship or a difficult situation within current relationships. The focus is to examine key, current issues that are related to the depression. Specific situations and alternative ways to cope are considered, sometimes with homework assignments. The IPT principle is that interpersonal difficulties often trigger depression, and the resolution of those difficulties will decrease depressive feelings. The therapist encourages the client to learn new and better ways of relating to people.

Let's see firsthand how IPT might work. Zoe had just had a baby, and the baby blues had definitely extended from a few days to months. Perhaps this was postpartum depression. Her husband told her that she needed to get help, or they might end up divorced. Zoe did a lot of crying, mostly because of her relationship with her mother-in-law, who lived with them for financial and social support (to care for the baby so that Zoe could return to work part-time). Her mother-in-law had a lot of ideas about how to raise a baby—after all, she'd raised eight of her own. Zoe and her mother-in-law disagreed about the importance of breastfeeding and having the baby on a sleep schedule. These disagreements turned into family fights, and Zoe ended up feeling deflated, worthless, and unheard by her mother-in-law and husband. In seeking help from an IPT therapist, Zoe was able to identify a few key goals. They began to work on her communication skills with her family and the doctor gave her ideas about how to approach them in a calm manner and develop compromises for the child-care situation. In a few months, Zoe could see the difference in her overall relationships at home and reported feeling less depressed and more in control.

PSYCHODYNAMIC THERAPY

Sometimes called *psychoanalytic psychotherapy*, *psychodynamic therapy* is the general name for a group of therapies that guide the client toward bringing unconscious (or what some might call subconscious) feelings and thoughts to the surface. Often these submerged feelings are initially too painful to be faced, and people use defenses to keep them at bay. These defenses may be causing harm, and once a client becomes aware of these defenses, the feelings may be less painful. Often there is a focus on childhood emotional injuries from parents or other important people. If these issues can be explored, the client might see connections in how relationships or experiences from the past inform relationships and experiences in the present. With insight, clients begin to feel better and make healthier choices that avoid reliving past patterns.

Not all psychodynamic therapists fully embrace Freud, who is the father of psychodynamic psychotherapy. Nor do all psychodynamic therapists have their clients lie on the couch, but most do believe that the past impacts the present. For example, Carol sought help from her doctor for several years.

164

She did so initially because of her severe PMS symptoms. Medication was somewhat helpful, but Carol knew there was more to her depression than just her menstrual cycle. With her doctor's help she began exploring her relationship with her mother, who had never valued her as a child. Carol's brother was considered the golden boy of the family, while Carol was a worthless girl. In some ways her period was tied to her mother's rejection. One of her strongest memories was when she was thirteen and got her first menses. She went to her mother for help, and her mother responded, "Well, here we go. Next thing you know, you will be moody and end up pregnant." Carol did not understand her mother's reaction, and during her adolescence she strived hard to be a tomboy—to ignore her femininity and to be as good as her brother. Now she's twenty-eight years old and wondering why she has yet to engage in any type of romantic relationship. With her doctor, she's starting down the long road to explore her self-image in relation to her mother's messages and the overall impact on her ability to explore a sexual and romantic relationship.

IMPACT

While this is hardly a comprehensive list of the psychotherapies available, it is at least an introduction to some very common types that have been used to treat depression. In terms of therapy's ability to improve depression, there have been hundreds of articles that emphasize the success of CBT. In some ways CBT is the easiest to research and study because there are very clear, easily defined goals. Symptoms of depression can be measured, and success can be claimed. In recent years, there has also been a focus on the success of IPT in treating depression, and some say it is just as effective as CBT. Most research has shown CBT or IPT to be as effective as medication (antidepressants), but research has also touted the importance of a combination approach (therapy and medication) for many women with hard-to-treat depression. Finally, there have been hundreds of successful case reports that address the miracles of psychodynamic therapy. In research it is harder to measure the outcome of this long-term therapy because it is so individualized in terms of therapist, client, and the journey of insight into the unconscious. Despite the sometimes controversial research on its immediate outcome, it can be an undeniably lifesaving approach for many people. No matter which therapy you choose, the important thing to remember is that if you are experiencing any type of mood changes related to estrogen imbalance, a therapist can help you. You will see a dramatic improvement if there is a good fit between you and your therapist.

Sleep Hygiene

When we talk about *sleep hygiene*, we are referring to your sleep habits and how they impact your ability to get a good night's sleep. We all know that little or poor sleep makes us feel irritable, have less energy, and have a harder time concentrating. As mentioned in chapter 5, we also know that sleep can be intimately tied to the estrogen-depression connection. Improving your sleep hygiene means targeting your habits to feel better physically and mentally. Suggestions to improve sleep include the following:

- Have a fixed bedtime.
- Avoid napping.
- Avoid alcohol four to six hours before bedtime.
- Avoid caffeine four to six hours before bedtime.
- Exercise regularly.
- Have comfortable bedding.
- Set the right temperature (cool is better).
- Eliminate noise.
- Reserve the bed for sleep and sex.
- Have a light snack, like warm milk, before bedtime.
- Try relaxation techniques.
- Try to put your worries aside.
- Take a warm shower or bath before bedtime.
- Read to relax.
- Choose the radio over television, if background noise is needed.

If you are having a hard time implementing these strategies or need help identifying what aspects of your sleep hygiene need to be improved, try consulting with a therapist. In particular, CBT therapists, as mentioned above, are usually trained to help you with sleep hygiene and can help you learn relaxation techniques and address the worries that might be keeping you up at night.

Western Medicine Again: Symptom Specific

In addition to lifestyle changes, we also need to turn to Western medicine for additional answers on how to treat some of the very specific symptoms that are associated with estrogen deficiency, particularly during the postmenopause phase of life. Sometimes natural supplements and/or some type of estrogen replacement (ERT or HRT) is not the ideal choice for addressing an estrogen-deficient symptom, like osteoporosis, heart disease, or even depression. Sometimes we need additional medication to obtain the best possible outcome. Let's take a look.

Osteoporosis

Almost 20 percent of a woman's bone loss occurs very quickly in the few years surrounding menopause, and bone loss continues if she does nothing to protect against it. If HRT is not the avenue for you, consider protecting yourself from osteoporosis by using a SERM (like Evista) or by using *bisphosphonate medications* (like Fosamax or Actonel), which are *antiresorptive* medications, meaning that they slow or stop the natural process that dissolves bone tissue. Recent research shows a reduction in fractures by 30 to 50 percent with these approaches (Castelo-Branco et al. 2005). As mentioned earlier, calcium and vitamin intake, along with proper diet and exercise, are also important. Dr. Delaney (2006) recently published an article that spoke of the best combination to protect against osteoporosis. The suggested combination includes a bisphosphonate medication or SERM, along with a balanced diet, good intake of vitamin D and calcium, regular exercise, fall prevention (assistance as needed), no smoking, and moderation of alcohol intake. Having a bone-density scan and getting proper consultation from your physician can help you to determine your risk and how to protect yourself.

Heart Disease

Because postmenopausal women are at ten times greater risk of dying from heart disease than from hip fractures or breast cancer, women need to consider protecting their hearts (Cummings, Black, and Rubin 1989). If you are concerned about increased risk of heart disease because of menopause and estrogen deficiency but do not feel that HRT is for you, consider other ways of protecting yourself. You might try *statin medications* (which control blood pressure and cholesterol), better diet, more exercise, and lifestyle changes, such as not smoking. This might be the best approach for you and your overall heart protection. Consult your doctor for a personal regimen that would benefit you the most.

Depression & Hot Flashes

In chapter 7, we talked about the importance of antidepressants as a well-established treatment for menopausal women, alleviating depression and often symptoms like hot flashes (Joffe et al. 2001; Soares, Poitras, and Prouty 2003; Cohen, Soares, and Joffe 2005). As we mentioned before, women beginning an antidepressant treatment typically feel an improvement in their mood within one month, and overall wellness is typically achieved if the woman remains on the antidepressant for at least six to twelve months (Cohen, Soares, and Joffe 2005). Antidepressants can reduce the occurrence of hot flashes by 50 to 60 percent (Stearns 2006), and this may be the safest option for those with breast cancer (Mom et al. 2006).

Additional Resources

In the past few years, some easy-to-read books have been published that can help you choose the right treatment for menopausal symptoms. We recommend taking a look at the following:

Perimenopause: Changes in Women's Health After 35, by Drs. Huston and Lanka (New Harbinger Publications 2001)

The Sexy Years, by Suzanne Somers (Random House 2004)

What Your Doctor May Not Tell You About Premenopause, by Drs. Lee, Hanley, and Hopkins (Warner Books 2004)

Natural Woman, Natural Menopause, by Marcus Laux and Christine Conrad (Harper Publishers 1998)

Conclusion

The ideal treatment approach to addressing your personal estrogen-depression connection depends on you. The goal is to have maximum health and vigor, both physically and mentally, as you age. This is probably best achieved with a combination of treatments and lifestyle changes. Think carefully about your own history, list the symptoms that bother you, and consult an expert. Consider fine-tuning your approach to estrogen deficiency in order to protect yourself and improve your overall well-being. This fine-tuning may include traditional or alternative choices for replacing estrogen, reducing stress, improving depression, eating right, and exercising regularly, just to mention a few.

It is our hope that these past few chapters have addressed some viable treatment options for you to consider as you come to better understand the estrogen-depression connection. We realize that no book can be exhaustive, and we are hopeful that science will continue to evolve and provide more data for all of us to consider. The goal is to promote mental health for women across a life span of development from birth to puberty to pregnancy to menopause. Improved quality of life is the aspiration. In the coming years, neuroscience is going to bring a host of changes, including newly tailored designer medications and herbal supplements that we hope will bring relief for those who will be addressing the estrogen-depression connection in their life.

CHAPTER 9

Conclusion

"Grandma, do you ever get sad?" The water gently swirled around Jeremiah's feet. He was wading in the pond, trying to catch one of the tadpoles that was brushing against his leg. Margaret was sitting next to him on the grassy shore, watching her grandson play. He had asked the question offhandedly, in the way children do, seemingly preoccupied with the activity at hand but concerned about something deeper.

Margaret paused for a second before she replied. "Sometimes I do, Jeremiah. Why do you ask?"

He made another lunge for a tadpole and came up empty-handed. "Sometimes my mom gets sad. I don't like it when she's sad."

Margaret's thoughts fluttered back to her own youth, recalling how she had had the blues even as a teenager. It was as if a black cloud would descend upon her for days, sometimes weeks. She remembered shutting out the world, escaping friends and family by reading, eating a carton of ice cream, or just burying herself in bed, crying herself to sleep. As she emerged from her teenage years and found success in school, dark clouds still plagued her. This darkness usually came monthly, and she remembered someone giving it the name "premenstrual syndrome." She learned how to cope with her PMS through psychotherapy, which her graduate school had required as part of becoming a marriage and family therapist. Therapy made a significant difference, but it was not until she had her first child that she considered taking medication. This child was the mother to whom Jeremiah was now referring.

"Sometimes, Jeremiah, sadness happens, even when you don't want it to. I'm sure your mom doesn't want to be sad, but it may be hard for her to control it. Don't you get sad or upset at times, even when you don't know why?"

Jeremiah had given up on the tadpoles and had moved on to trying to catch some of the younger frogs. But, they were a bit too quick and agile for him.

"Yeah, but I'm not a grown-up."

"Grown-ups can get sad, too."

"Even grandmas?"

"Why sure, even grandmas."

Margaret remembered being thirty-two, pregnant with her daughter Joy (Jeremiah's mom) and how excited she was to have a baby on the way. What she did not expect were the weeks and months following the arrival of her daughter. She remembered being blown away by the postpartum depression she'd experienced. Her world had begun to crumble. She'd felt little attachment to her newborn daughter; she hadn't been able to reach out and connect with her husband; and returning to her private practice had seemed like an impossible goal. She remembered that she'd needed help fast, so after seeking a psychiatry consultation, she began taking an antidepressant and went back to individual psychotherapy. Within three months she'd felt significantly better, and within six months she had returned to feeling like her old self.

The next time that she hit "rock bottom" was some years later. It was at around age fifty that menopause snuck up on her. She endured several rough months of hot flashes and sleep disturbances, not to mention extreme irritability and family fighting. Once again, she'd sought help, but this time it was from a gynecologist who was well versed in an estrogen-based treatment approach. Because she had no family history of breast cancer, and because Margaret was going through menopause naturally, she was told that a combination of estrogen and progesterone was best for her. She also wanted some immediate relief from her mood swings, so she went back on a combination of Prozac and hormone replacement therapy (HRT). After two years, she stopped the Prozac, but she continued on HRT for another three years to give her an extra edge of control over her postmenopausal symptoms. It was just last year, at age fifty-seven, that she'd felt stable enough to go without any medication.

"You know, Jeremiah, sometimes things happen in the bodies of girls that make them sad for awhile. It can happen in boys and men too, but sometimes it happens more in girls because of things they can't control, because of real changes in their bodies. It's nothing for you to worry about, but just know that some times are harder than others for moms and for girls."

"Does everybody know this, Grandma? Maybe it's important for all boys and girls to know this. It might make it easier for girls."

Jeremiah leapt onto the shore and reached for a big bullfrog. "Look, Grandma, I got it!" He proudly held up the frog so all the world could see.

"Yes, you did!"

Inside, Margaret smiled proudly and thought, *Yes, you did*.

Accepting the Estrogen-Depression Connection

Margaret's story typifies what the estrogen-depression connection is truly about. There are clear points in the lives of many women when they are vulnerable to an increased risk for depression. These points are usually developmental milestones and correlate with reproductive stages, when estrogen levels are fluctuating, leaving the female brain more susceptible to depression and other mood changes. If you ask most women about the relationship between estrogen and mood, many would probably acknowledge that there is a connection, recognizing how estrogen can impact how a woman thinks and feels. And most women would feel comfortable saying this because they are thinking of key reproductive stages such as PMS, postpartum depression, or menopause when estrogen may have influenced their own lives.

Women might acknowledge that this relationship exists, but many may not appreciate how *strong* this connection really is. It is often not until a woman gains Margaret's perspective, the perspective of a woman looking back on her life, that she may be able to fully appreciate how much of her mood and emotional functioning really depended on what was happening with the estrogen levels in her body. From the vantage point of looking backward, seeing the trajectory of your emotional transformation, it is easier to place your pain, sadness, and despair in context.

For those who do not have this retrospective vantage point, however, it may be difficult to accept the strength of the relationship between estrogen and mood. In particular, it may be difficult because it seems to undercut a sense of responsibility and personal emotional control. Many women see estrogen as a biological phenomenon that is beyond their immediate control so that linking it with mood may feel like putting emotions into the same biological and therefore uncontrollable camp. One of the many gifts of science and research on the biochemistry of the brain is an understanding of how much depression, anxiety, and emotional functioning depend on biology. Yet many women may find it difficult to accept this biological basis for depression because there is an inherent pressure to see depression as something that they can directly control or change by thinking or acting in a new way. While it is true that there is power in positive thinking, and that changing your thoughts or actions toward positive ends can elevate mood, there is also a strong biological and hormonal component that can operate outside of our immediate control.

Why can this lack of direct responsibility for one's emotions be an uncomfortable notion? If you think about it, the lives of women are focused on having responsibility, simply out of necessity. From early on, many girls are taught to behave differently than boys, to act with more propriety and responsibility rather than with recklessness and carelessness. In school, young girls are consistently encouraged to perform well academically *and* concurrently lead an active extracurricular life in sports, dance, music, or drama. Many women are enduring the demands and responsibility of college, and others are proceeding to graduate school. At the same time, they are working to pay their bills, and they are often responsible for raising their families in ways that many men are "inoculated" against. Women give birth, provide milk, change diapers, put on bandages, help with homework, and provide a listening ear to their children, loving them to the point of letting them go when they reach adulthood. And they are also more likely than men to be the primary caregivers for their aging parents. Women really do assume a lot of responsibility, so it is not surprising that they may find it difficult to accept that their mood can be beyond their immediate control.

The Take-Home Message

The thrust of this book has been to highlight how much a woman's mood can fluctuate according to the changes in estrogen that are occurring in her body and brain. The heart of this book can perhaps be best captured with this sentence:

Depression can occur in a subset of susceptible women
as a result of natural fluctuations in estrogen levels
associated with the developmental stages of a woman's life.

Let's break this sentence down into sections.

Depression can occur in a subset of susceptible women . . .

One of the things that we have tried to emphasize is that depression does not occur in all women. As we learned earlier, women are about twice as likely as men to experience depression at some point in their lives, but this does not mean that all women will experience the full symptoms of a major depressive disorder. However, there is a group of women who will develop depression, and this is likely due to a certain susceptibility, vulnerability, or predisposition. The factors that create this vulnerability are varied, including genetic and environmental factors. Women who have mothers or other relatives with depression are at a significantly higher risk for developing depression themselves. Similarly, women who have high levels of emotional stress, whether it be attachment difficulties with a child, the recent loss of a loved one, or difficult work environments, are also more likely to develop depression.

. . . as a result of natural fluctuations in estrogen levels . . .

For many women, however, this vulnerability or increased susceptibility to depression is created and/or enhanced by their response to a natural change

174

in estrogen levels. These changes are ordinary and inherent to the menstrual cycle. In fact, there would be no menstrual cycle without these changes, so it is important to note that these changes are natural and expected for every woman.

This is important because many women feel alienated and estranged from their bodies during depression. They may be ashamed by what they perceive to be their imperfections, wishing they could change their weight or some facial feature, or they may feel somewhat victimized by their bodies, which seem to be merely carrying them along for the ride. But it is essential to recognize that estrogen fluctuations in themselves are not the culprit for depression. If this was true, then every woman, and perhaps every man for that matter, would develop depression because both women and men experience natural changes in estrogen levels throughout their life spans.

So if these estrogen changes themselves are not the culprit for depression, what is? Most likely it is a woman's response or sensitivity to these changes. There does not appear to be any quantitative difference in the actual levels of estrogen in a woman's body and brain between those who develop and do not develop depression. But some women have an unusual response to these natural changes such that it lowers their threshold for developing depression. These changes have a psychologically destabilizing action that renders the female brain more vulnerable to developing sadness, loss of pleasure, and reductions in the quality of appetite and sleep. In a sense, then, the depression that many women experience may be a distinct response to a natural hormonal change.

. . . associated with the developmental stages of a woman's life.

And these hormonal changes appear to be related to reproductive transitions. It is at the significant stages of a woman's reproductive life cycle that these hormonal changes occur, initiating a sequence of events that can result in depression for a subset of women. Although estrogen can fluctuate at various times, it is during puberty and premenstrual, postpartum, and menopausal phases that the most significant fluctuations occur. During the middle of puberty, adolescent girls are exposed to monthly surges of estrogen, disrupting normal hormonal balance and kindling larger changes in mood.

This leaves adolescent girls particularly susceptible to feeling gloomy and self-critical, withdrawing from pleasurable activities, and experiencing observable changes in appetite, loss of energy, and disrupted sleep. For women with PMS, the drop in estrogen and rise in progesterone in the final (luteal) phase of the menstrual cycle can be associated with depression, irritability, anxiety, confusion, social withdrawal, and angry outbursts. When women give birth and the placenta is removed at delivery, the estrogen levels that have built up during pregnancy drop dramatically, typically lower than would be expected if the reproductive organs failed. It is this rise and fall of estrogen, this dramatic change in the hormonal environment, that can account for the mild and temporary sadness of the "baby blues," the full symptoms of postpartum depression, and the more severe and serious symptoms of psychosis, mania, and disorganized behavior in postpartum psychosis. Furthermore, the fluctuation and decline in ovarian hormone production during perimenopause, as well as the cessation of menstruation in menopause and the absence of estrogen production in postmenopause, can trigger additional symptoms or episodes of depression. Hence, many episodes of depression in women seem to pivot around key moments of hormonal change.

The female brain appears to be biologically constructed toward greater sensitivity to these fluctuations in estrogen. Even prior to birth, there are organizational operations that modify the brain structure and neural circuitry in a way that differentiates the female body, brain, and neurodevelopment from those of the male. This includes the unique placement of a high density of receptors for estrogen in the brain structures that are responsible for emotional processing and mood, such as the limbic system. Estrogen exerts a second and activational operation on the female brain following birth, altering the availability of several biochemical messengers involved in the regulation of mood, including dopamine, norepinephrine, acetylcholine, glutamate, GABA, and serotonin. By controlling the creation, release, and breakdown of these neurotransmitters, estrogen acts in a way that is similar to antidepressants. In a sense, women's brains are more vulnerable to developing depression in part because their brains are more sensitive than men's brains to changes in estrogen levels.

Making It Personal

Regardless of the technical explanations, it is most important to recognize the strength of the relationship between estrogen and depression, how this connection is strongest during times of reproductive transition, and how it is in part biologically fixed in the brains of women, making some women particularly vulnerable to developing depression. The next question becomes what to do with this knowledge and how to incorporate it into your own life.

Even if you are among those women who do not notice symptoms of depression during the times of estrogen fluctuation, it is important for you to carefully examine both your current and prior symptoms of depression. It is often helpful to construct a list of both your emotional and physical symptoms. This includes asking yourself if you have depressed mood, hopelessness, loss of pleasure in previously enjoyable activities, appetite or weight changes, sleep problems, fatigue or loss of energy, feelings of worthlessness or guilt, or even thoughts about death.

Next, it is critical to examine these symptoms in the context of your own family history and the developmental phases of your life. If you know that your mother, grandmother, or other female member of your family struggled with depression, then your risk is likely to be greater. However, by knowing when they struggled with it (that is, if it was during menopause or a postpartum period) and how they treated it, this information can be used for your own treatment and for determining the possible contribution of estrogen to your own depressive symptoms. It is also important to keep in perspective the times or occasions when depression seems to arise for you. Is it around the premenstrual phase of your menstrual cycle? Did it appear in puberty or the postpartum period? Are you in the stages of perimenopause and experiencing depression, but have not yet linked the two? Many women find it particularly helpful to journal or keep a log of their depressive symptoms and when they occur.

It is critical to then consult with your health care professional about these symptoms. This professional can take a thorough life history, place your symptoms in the context of your other medical conditions, review your history of depression, and explore how you responded to earlier life transitions, which could help determine if you are at risk for future episodes of depression. Health care professionals can rule out other medical conditions that can mask as depression, such as hypothyroidism, anemia, sleep apnea, and vascular conditions like high blood pressure and high cholesterol. Even if you feel like you are not currently experiencing any signs of depression, it is important to discuss your risk with your physician.

For those women who are experiencing depression, part of their consultation with their physician should include exploring possible treatment options. Selective serotonin reuptake inhibitors (SSRIs) have emerged as a first line of defense against depression due to their low side effects, the relative ease in getting a prescription, and their safety in the event of an overdose. There is even some research suggesting that women respond better than men to SSRIs, possibly because SSRIs can reverse adverse effects of estrogen fluctuation on serotonin levels. However, women in postmenopause and postpartum depression, as well as those with treatment-resistant depression, may be less responsive to SSRIs, making these women better candidates for HRT. This highlights the importance of examining and selecting treatment options in light of your developmental or reproductive phase.

As we discussed in chapter 8, some women find it helpful to pair these pharmacological interventions with alternative treatment options, such as bio-identical estrogens, herbal supplements, lifestyle changes, and psychotherapy. Many of these alternative approaches are helpful for all women. Exercise, improved sleep, reduced stress, and healthier eating can all be natural anti-depressants. Psychotherapy can be extremely helpful in altering thought patterns, changing relationships, and exploring the impact of the past so that changes in the present can be made. This process can alleviate depression and substitute healthier modes of approaching yourself and others. The efficacy of some of these alternative approaches, such as SERMs, is not fully documented and may be different for each woman, but physicians can be critically helpful in determining if they may be right for you.

When confronted with these multiple options, many women ask how to decide among them. Although there is no magical formula, it may be helpful to first try traditional treatment approaches, such as SSRIs or HRT, because they have been scientifically supported. However, if these traditional approaches do not seem appropriate for some reason, maybe it is best to consider alternative treatment options. Even if you are using traditional approaches, many women find it helpful to combine them with alternative treatments, like taking Prozac while pursuing psychotherapy, using natural supplements, and developing a healthier lifestyle by eating better and exercising more. A combination of treatments and lifestyle adjustments can help a woman to achieve her best physical and mental health.

Conclusion: Destigmatizing Depression

Unfortunately, the grim reality is that very few women actually pursue treatment for depression. When the symptoms of depression first manifest, many women go to a primary care physician and present with physical symptoms, saying they have low energy, reduced sexual drive, and poor attention and concentration. Even more unfortunate is the reality that many health care professionals overlook depression as a possible explanation for these symptoms. In fact, fewer than one-third of depressed women get treatment (Downey 1999). This discourages many women from discussing their symptoms, especially because they feel like their symptoms may be overlooked or dismissed. However, this does not mean that women should be deterred. It is your pain, your tearfulness, and your lack of energy that deserve attention and that can be treated. The difficulty is that it is too easy to leave the decisions about depression to others, letting them determine whether your symptoms are significant or not. Frequently, women tell us that they did not report depression because they did not want to bother their doctor or thought their symptoms were insignificant as compared to the struggles of their partner or children. However, pursuing treatment not only encourages personal health but also the health of your relationships.

Depression and estrogen-related issues need to be destigmatized to the point that it feels okay to ask for help. When Tipper Gore, wife of Vice President Al Gore, disclosed her own episode of depression in 1991, it was immediately perceived as a campaign ploy. In a sense, depression and estrogen-related mood changes are seen either as things that women use to their advantage or as liabilities. The old saying, "It's just her time of the month," comes to mind. However, the more that depression is kept in the closet—that is, the more that we overlook the strong connection between estrogen and depression—the less of an opportunity there is for women to be free of their depression.

Perhaps the connection between estrogen and depression will be better communicated if it is a rallying point for women. Over the past several years, there has been a large mustering of support and a sense of bonding for women around the issue of breast cancer. Women attend conferences and gather for marathons that center on breast cancer. They ask each other about breast cancer and explicitly encourage each other to engage in assessment and prevention. If women can rally around the estrogen-depression connection in the same way that they have rallied around breast cancer, depression and estrogen-related mood changes could become a source of community and solidarity rather than isolation and silence. Many women find it easy to talk about the effects of estrogen, such as PMS or menopause, on their lives. These shared experiences can help them develop a sense of community and closeness with other women. But this sense of connection and solidarity is mysteriously absent when it comes to the impact of estrogen on depression. Maybe it is partially due to lack of knowledge, which is why it is so important for older women to teach younger women, and for women in general to teach men, about the strong connection between estrogen and depression. Armed with this knowledge, perhaps the link between estrogen and depression can be used to explore the protective effects of estrogen, providing women with a new resource for emotional well-being.

References

ACOG (American College of Obstetricians and Gynecologists). 2000. Premenstrual syndrome. *ACOG Practice Bulletin*, no. 15, 1–12. Washington, DC: American College of Obstetricians and Gynecologists.

Adams, K. F., A. Schatzkin, T. B. Harris, V. Kipnis, T. Mouw, R. Ballard-Barbash, A. Hollenbeck, and M. F. Leitzmann. 2006. Overweight, obesity, and mortality in a large prospective cohort of persons 50 to 71 years old. *New England Journal of Medicine* 355(8): 758–760.

Ahokas, A., M. Aito, and S. Turiainen. 2000. Association between oestradiol and puerperal psychosis. *Acta Psychiatrica Scandinavica* 101:167–170.

Ahokas, A., J. Kaukoranta, K. Wahlbeck, and M. Aito. 2001. Estrogen deficiency in severe postpartum depression: Successful treatment with sublingual physiologic 17-estradiol: A preliminary study. *Journal of Clinical Psychiatry* 62(5): 332–336.

Alexander, J. L., K. Kotz, L. Dennerstein, and S. Davis. 2004. What do the randomized control trials tell us about the treatment of libido in the symptomatic postmenopausal woman? Program and abstracts from the 2nd World Congress of Women's Mental Health, Washington, DC (March 7–10).

Alexopoulos, G. S., B. S. Meyers, R. C. Young, B. Kalayam, T. Kakuma, M. Gabrielle, J. A. Sirey, and J. Hull. 2000. Executive dysfunction and long-term outcomes of geriatric depression. *Archives of General Psychiatry* 57: 285–290.

Amin, Z., T. Canli, and C. N. Epperson. 2005. Effect of estrogen-serotonin interactions on mood and cognition. *Behavioral and Cognitive Neuroscience Reviews* 4(1): 43–58.

Amy, J. J. 2005. Hormones and menopause: Pro. *Acta Clinica Belgica* 60(5): 261–268.

Angold, A., E. J. Costello, A. Erkanli, and C. M. Worthman. 1999. Pubertal changes in hormone levels and depression in girls. *Psychological Medicine* 29: 1043–1053.

Angold, A., E. J. Costello, and C. M. Worthman. 1998. Puberty and depression: The roles of age, pubertal status and pubertal timing. *Psychological Medicine* 28: 51–61.

APA (American Psychiatric Association). 1994. *Diagnostic and Statistical Manual of Mental Disorders*, 4th ed. Washington, DC: American Psychiatric Association.

Archer, J. S. M. 1999. Relationship between estrogen, serotonin, and depression. *Menopause: Journal of the North American Menopause Society* 6: 71–78.

Arpels, J. C. 1996. The female brain hypoestrogenic continuum from the premenstrual syndrome to menopause: A hypothesis and review of supporting data. *Journal of Reproductive Medicine* 41: 633–639.

Avis, N. E., D. Brambilla, S. M. McKinlay, and K. Vass. 1994. A longitudinal analysis of the association between menopause and depression: Results from the Massachusetts Women's Health Study. *Annals of Epidemiology* 4: 214–220.

Avis, N. E., S. Brockwell, and A. Colvin. 2005. A universal menopausal syndrome? *American Journal of Medicine* 118(12, suppl. 2): 37S–46S.

Avis, N. E., P. A. Kaufert, M. Lock, S. M. McKinlay, and K. Vass. 1993. The evolution of menopausal symptoms. *Bailliere's Clinical Endocrinology and Metabolism* 7(1): 17–32.

Avis, N. E., and S. M. McKinlay. 1991. A longitudinal analysis of women's attitudes toward the menopause: Results from the Massachusetts Women's Health Study. *Maturitas* 13: 65–79.

Backstrom, T., L. Andreen, V. Birzniece, I. Bjorn, I. M. Johansson, M. Nordenstam-Haghjo, S. Nyberg, I. Sundstrom-Poromaa, G. Wahlstrom, M. Wang, and D. Zhu. 2003. The role of hormones and hormonal treatments in premenstrual syndrome. *CNS Drugs* 17(5): 325–342.

Barnhart, K. T., E. Freeman, J. A. Grisso, D. J. Rader, M. Sammel, S. Kapoor, and L. W. Nestler. 1999. The effect of dehydroepiandrosterone supplementation to symptomatic perimenopausal women on serum endocrine profiles, lipid parameters, and health-related quality of life. *Journal of Clinical Endocrinology and Metabolism* 84(11): 3896–3902.

Bennett, D. S., P. J. Ambrosini, D. Kudes, C. Metz, and H. Rabinovich. 2005. Gender differences in adolescent depression: Do symptoms differ for boys and girls? *Journal of Affective Disorders* 89: 35–44.

Bloch, M., P. J. Schmidt, M. Danaceau, J. Murphy, L. Nieman, and D. R. Rubinow. 2000. Effects of gonadal steroids in women with a history of postpartum depression. *American Journal of Psychiatry* 157: 924–930.

Bromley, S. E., C. S. de Vries, D. Thomas, and R. D. Farmer. 2005. Hormone replacement therapy and risk of acute myocardial infarction: A review of the literature. *Drug Safety* 28(6): 473–493.

Butters, M. A., J. T. Becher, R. D. Nebes, M. D. Zmuda, B. H. Mulsant, B. G. Pollock, and C. F. Reynolds. 2000. Changes in cognitive functioning following treatment of late-life depression. *American Journal of Psychiatry* 157(12): 1949–1954.

Campbell, S., and M. Whitehead. 1977. Oestrogen therapy and the menopausal syndrome. *Clinics in Obstetrics and Gynaecology* 4: 31–47.

Carlson, L. E., and B. B. Sherwin. 1998. Steroid hormones, memory and mood in a healthy elderly population. *Psychoneuroendocrinology* 23: 583–603.

Castelo-Branco, C., S. Palacios, J. Calaf, F. Vazquez, and J. L. Lanchares. 2005. Available medical choices for the management of menopause. *Maturitas* 52(suppl. 1): S61–S70.

Chakravorty, S. G., and U. Halbreich. 1997. The influence of estrogen on monoamine oxidase activity. *Psychopharmacology Bulletin* 33(2): 229–233.

Cohen, L. S., C. N. Soares, and H. Joffe. 2005. Diagnosis and management of mood disorders during the menopausal transition. *American Journal of Medicine* 118(12, suppl. 2): 93–97.

Cohen, R. M., P. J. Andreason, and T. Sunderland. 1997. The ratio of mesial to neocortical temporal lobe blood flow as a predictor of dementia. *Journal of the American Geriatrics Society* 45(3): 329–333.

Cooper, C. 1997. The crippling consequences of fractures and their impact on quality of life. *American Journal of Medicine* 103(2, suppl. 1): 12S–19S.

Costa, M. M., V. I. Reus, O. M. Wolkowitz, F. Manfredi, and M. Lieberman. 1999. Estrogen replacement therapy and cognitive decline in memory-impaired post-menopausal women. *Biological Psychiatry* 46(2): 182–188.

Crane, H. M., S. E. Van Rompaey, and M. M. Kitahata. 2006. Antiretroviral medications associated with elevated blood pressure among patients receiving highly active antiretroviral therapy. *AIDS* 20(7): 1019–1026.

Cranney, A., and J. D. Adachi. 2005. Benefit-risk assessment of raloxifene in postmenopausal osteoporosis. *Drug Safety* 28(8): 721–730.

Cummings, J. A., and L. Brizendine. 2002. Comparison of physical and emotional side effects of progesterone or medroxyprogesterone in early postmenopausal women. *Menopause: Journal of the North American Menopause Society* 9: 253–263.

Cummings, S. R., D. M. Black, and S. M. Rubin. 1989. Lifetime risks of hip, Colles', or vertebral fracture and coronary heart disease among white postmenopausal women. *Archives of Internal Medicine* 149(11): 2445–2448.

Dal Forno, G., M. T. Palermo, J. E. Donohue, H. Karagiozis, A. B. Zonderman, and C. H. Kawas. 2005. Depressive symptoms, sex and risk for Alzheimer's disease. *Annals of Neurology* 57: 381–387.

Dayal, M., M. D. Sammel, J. Zhao, A. C. Hummel, K. Vandenbourne, and K. T. Barnhart. 2005. Supplementation with DHEA: Effect on muscle size, strength, quality of life, and lipids. *Journal of Women's Health* 14(5): 391–400.

DeKosky, S. T., A. Fitzpatrick, D. G. Ives, J. Saxton, J. Williamson, O. L. Lopez, G. Burke, L. Fried, L. H. Kuller, J. Robbins, R. Tracy, N. Woolard, L. Dunn, R. Kronmal, R. Nahin, C. Furberg, for GEMS Investigators. 2006. The Ginkgo Evaluation of Memory (GEM) study: Design and baseline data of a randomized trial of Ginkgo biloba extract in prevention of dementia. *Contemporary Clinical Trials* 27: 238–253.

Delaney, M. F. 2006. Strategies for the prevention and treatment of osteoporosis during early postmenopause. *American Journal of Obstetrics and Gynecology* 194(2 suppl.): S12–S23.

Dennerstein, L., G. Gotts, J. B. Brown, C. A. Morse, T. M. M. Farley, and A. Pinol. 1994. The relationship between the menstrual cycle and female sexual interest in women with PMS complaints and volunteers. *Psychoneuroendocrinology* 19(3): 293–304.

Dennis, C. E. 2004. Preventing postpartum depression part I: A review of biological interventions. *Canadian Journal of Psychiatry* 49(7): 467–475.

Dennis, C. E., and D. E. Stewart. 2004. Treatment of postpartum depression, part 1: A critical review of biological interventions. *Journal of Clinical Psychiatry* 65(9): 1242–1251.

Desai, H. D., and M. W. Jann. 2000. Major depression in women: A review of the literature. *Journal of the American Pharmaceutical Association* 40(4): 525–537.

DeWaele, B., B. Vanmierlo, Y. Van Nieuwenhove, and G. Delvaux. 2006. Impact of body overweight and class I, II and III obesity on the outcome of acute biliary pancreatitis. *Pancreas* 32(4): 343–345.

Dickerson, L. M., P. J. Mazyck, and M. H. Hunter. 2003. Premenstrual syndrome. *American Family Physician* 67(8): 1743–1752.

Downey, J. I. 1999. Recognizing the range of mood disorders in women. *Medscape General Medicine* 1(1). Retrieved from http://www.medscape .com/viewarticle/408809.

Duff, S. J., and E. Hampson. 2000. A beneficial effect of estrogen on working memory in postmenopausal women taking hormone replacement therapy. *Hormones and Behavior* 38: 262–276.

Dunkin, J., N. Rasgon, M. Zeller, K. Wagner-Steh, S. David, L. Altshuler, and A. Rapkin. 2006. Estrogen replacement and cognition in postmenopausal women: Effect of years since menopause on response to treatment. *Drug Development Research* 66: 150–159.

Dzaja, A., S. Arber, J. Hislop, M. Kerkhofs, C. Kopp, T. Pollmacher, P. Polo-Kantola, D. J. Skene, I. Tobler, and T. Porkka-Heiskanen. 2005. Women's sleep in health and disease. *Journal of Psychiatric Research* 39: 55–76.

Eberling, J. L., B. R. Reed, J. E. Coleman, and W. J. Jagust. 2000. Effect of estrogen on cerebral glucose metabolism in postmenopausal women. *Neurology* 55(6): 875–877.

Egger, H. L., E. J. Costello, A. Erkanli, and A. Angold. 1999. Somatic complaints and psychopathology in children and adolescents: Stomach aches, musculoskeletal pains, and headaches. *Journal of the American Academy of Child and Adolescent Psychiatry* 38: 852–860.

Elderkin-Thompson, V., A. Kumar, J. Mintz, K. Boone, E. Bahng, and H. Lavretsky. 2004. Executive dysfunction and visuospatial ability among depressed elders in a community setting. *Archives of Clinical Neuropsychology* 19: 597–611.

EMEA (The European Agency for the Evaluation of Medicinal Products). 2003. *EMEA public statement on recent publications regarding hormone replacement therapy.* Post-authorisation evaluation of medicines for human use (conference), London (December 3).

Eriksson, E., B. Andersch, H. P. Ho, M. Landen, and C. Sundblad. 2002. Diagnosis and treatment of premenstrual dysphoria. *Journal of Clinical Psychiatry* 63 (suppl. 7): 6–23.

Eriksson, O., T. Backstrom, M. Stridsberg, M. Hammarlund-Udenaes, and T. Naessen. 2006. Differential response to estrogen challenge test in women with and without premenstrual dysphoria. *Psychoneuroendocrinology* 31: 415–427.

Fink, G., B. E. H. Sumner, R. Rosie, O. Grace, and J. P. Quinn. 1996. Estrogen control of central neurotransmission: Effect on mood, mental state and memory. *Cellular and Molecular Neurobiology* 16 (3): 325–344.

Fisher, B., J. P. Costantino, D. L. Wickerham, C. K. Redmond, M. Kavanah, W. M. Cronin, V. Vogel, A. Robidoux, N. Dimitrov, J. Atkins, M. Daly, S. Wieand, E. Tan-Chiu, L. Ford, and N. Wolmark. 1998. Tamoxifen for prevention of breast cancer: Report of the National Surgical Adjuvant Breast and Bowel Project P-1 Study. *Journal of the National Cancer Institute* 90 (18): 1371–1388.

Flegal, K. M., B. I. Graubard, D. F. Williamson, and M. H. Gail. 2005. Excess deaths associated with underweight, overweight, and obesity. *Journal of the American Medical Association* 293 (15): 1861–1867.

Francucci, C. M., P. Daniele, N. Iori, A. Camilletti, F. Massi, and M. Boscaro. 2005. Effects of raloxifene on body fat distribution and lipid profile in healthy post-menopausal women. *Journal of Endocrinological Investigation* 28 (7): 623–631.

Freeman, E. W., M. D. Sammel, H. Lin, C. R. Gracia, S. Kapoor, and T. Ferdousi. 2005. The role of anxiety and hormonal changes in menopausal hot flashes. *Menopause: Journal of the North American Menopause Society* 12 (3): 258–266.

Freeman, E. W., M. D. Sammel, H. Lin, and D. B. Nelson. 2006. Associations of hormones and menopausal status with depressed mood in women with no history of depression. *Archives of General Psychiatry* 63 (4): 375–382.

Freeman, E. W., M. D. Sammel, L. Liu, C. R. Gracia, D. B. Nelson, and L. Hollander. 2004. Hormones and menopausal status as predictors of depression in women in transition to menopause. *Archives of General Psychiatry* 61 (1): 62–70.

Garbe, E., L. Levesque, and S. Suissa. 2004. Variability of breast cancer risk in observational studies of hormone replacement therapy: A meta-regression analysis. *Maturitas* 47(3): 175–183.

Geiss, L. S., L. Pan, B. Cadwell, E. W. Gregg, S. M. Benjamin, and M. M. Engelgau. 2006. Changes in incidence of diabetes in U.S. adults, 1997–2003. *American Journal of Preventive Medicine* 30(5): 371–377.

Genazzani, A. D., M. Stomati, F. Bernardi, M. Pieri, L. Rovati, and A. R. Genazzani. 2003. Long-term low-dose dehydroepiandrosterone oral supplementation in early and late postmenopausal women modulates endocrine parameters and synthesis of neuroactive steroids. *Fertility and Sterility* 80(6): 1495–1501.

Greene, R. A., and W. Dixon. 2002. The role of reproductive hormones in maintaining cognition. *Obstetrics and Gynecology Clinics of North America* 29: 437–453.

Greerlings, M. I., R. A. Schoevers, A. T. F. Beekman, C. Jonker, D. J. H. Deeg, B. Schmand, H. J. Ader, L. M. Bouter, and W. van Tilburg. 2000. Depression and risk of cognitive decline and Alzheimer's disease. *British Journal of Psychiatry* 176: 568–575.

Halbreich, U. 2000. Gonadal hormones, reproductive age, and women with depression. *Archives of General Psychiatry* 57(12): 1163–1164.

———. 2003. The etiology, biology, and evolving pathology of premenstrual syndromes. *Psychoneuroendocrinology* 28: 55–99.

Halbreich, U., and L. S. Kahn. 2001. Role of estrogen in the aetiology and treatment of mood disorders. *CNS Drugs* 15(10): 797–817.

Hardy, R., and D. Kuh. 1999. Reproductive characteristics and the age at inception of the perimenopause in a British national cohort. *American Journal of Epidemiology* 149: 612–620.

Hauenstein, E. J. 2003. Depression in adolescence. *Journal of Obstetric, Gynecological, and Neonatal Nursing* 32: 239–248.

Hay, A. G., J. Bancroft, and E. C. Johnstone. 1994. Affective symptoms in women attending a menopause clinic. *British Journal of Psychiatry* 164: 513–516.

Hays, J., J. K. Ockene, R. L. Brunner, J. M. Kotchen, J. E. Manson, R. E. Patterson, A. K. Aragaki, S. A. Shumaker, R. G. Brzyski, A. Z. LaCroix, I. A. Granek, and B. G. Valanis. 2003. Effects of estrogen plus progestin on health-related quality of life. *New England Journal of Medicine* 348: 1839–1854.

Hayward, C., and K. Sanborn. 2002. Puberty and the emergence of gender differences in psychopathology. *Journal of Adolescent Health* 30(4, suppl. 1): 49–58.

Henderson, V. W., L. Watt, and J. G. Buckwalter. 1996. Cognitive skills associated with estrogen replacement in women with Alzheimer's disease. *Psychoneuroendocrinology* 21: 421–430.

Hendrick, V., L. Altshuler, and R. Suri. 1998. Hormonal changes in the postpartum and implications for postpartum depression. *Psychosomatics* 39: 93–101.

Hlatky, M. D., D. Boothroyd, E. Vitinghoff, P. Sharp, and M. A. Whooley. 2002. Quality-of-life and depressive symptoms in postmenopausal women after receiving hormone therapy: Results from the Heart and Estrogen/Progestin Replacement Study (HERS) trial. *Journal of the American Medical Association* 287(5): 591–597.

Huston, J. E., and D. Lanka. 2001. *Perimenopause: Changes in Women's Health After 35.* Oakland, CA: New Harbinger Publications, Inc.

Huston, S., B. Sleath, and R. H. Rubin. 2001. Physician gender and hormone replacement therapy discussion. *Journal of Women's Health and Gender-based Medicine* 10(3): 279–287.

Huttner, R. P., and J. E. Shepherd. 2003. Gonadal steroids, selective serotonin reuptake inhibitors, and mood disorders in women. *Medical Clinics of North America* 87: 1065–1076.

Janssen, I., P. T. Katzmarzyk, and R. Ross. 2005. Body mass index is inversely related to mortality in older people after adjustment for waist circumference. *Journal of the American Geriatrics Society* 53(12): 2112–2118.

Jaskiewicz, K., S. Raczynska, R. Rzepko, and Z. Sledzinski. 2006. Nonalcoholic fatty liver disease treated by gastroplasty. *Digestive Diseases and Sciences* 51(1): 21–26.

Joffe, H., and L. S. Cohen. 1998. Estrogen, serotonin, and mood disturbance: Where is the therapeutic bridge? *Biological Psychiatry* 44: 798–811.

Joffe, H., H. Groninger, C. N. Soares, R. Nonacs, and L. S. Cohen. 2001. An open trial of mirtazapine in menopausal women with depression unresponsive to estrogen replacement therapy. *Journal of Women's Health and Gender-based Medicine* 10(10): 999–1004.

Judd, H. J. 1996. The impact of ovarian hormone replacement on selected risk factors of coronary heart disease. *Menopausal Medicine* 4(1): 9–11.

Kaltiala-Heino, R., E. Kosunen, and M. Rimpela. 2003. Pubertal timing, sexual behaviour and self-reported depression in middle adolescence. *Journal of Adolescence* 26: 531–545.

Kaltiala-Heino, R., M. Marttunen, P. Rantanen, and M. Rimpela. 2003. Early puberty is associated with mental health problems in middle adolescence. *Social Science and Medicine* 57: 1055–1064.

Kawas, C., S. Resnick, A. Morrison, R. Brookmeyer, M. Corrada, A. Zonderman, C. Bacal, D. D. Lingle, and E. Metter. 1997. A prospective study of estrogen replacement therapy and the risk of developing Alzheimer's disease: The Baltimore Longitudinal Study of Aging. *Neurology* 48: 1517–1521.

Kendler, K. S., L. M. Karkowski, L. A. Corey, and M. C. Neale. 1998. Longitudinal population-based twin study of retrospectively reported premenstrual symptoms and lifetime major depression. *American Journal of Psychiatry* 155(9): 1234–1240.

Kendler, K. S., J. L. Silberg, M. C. Neale, R. C. Kessler, A. C. Heath, and L. J. Eaves. 1992. Genetic and environmental factors in the aetiology of menstrual, premenstrual and neurotic symptoms: A population-based twin study. *Psychological Medicine* 22(1): 85–100.

Kernan, C., K. J. Miller, C. Genest, P. Siddarth, L. Ercoli, and G. W. Small. 2005. Cognitive profile during perimenopause: Parallels to post-menopause? *Journal of the International Neuropsychological Society* 11:189.

Kimura, D. 1995. Estrogen replacement therapy may protect against intellectual decline. *Hormones and Behavior* 29: 312–321.

Klein, B. E., R. Klein, S. C. Jensen, and L. L. Ritter. 1994. Are sex hormones associated with age-related maculopathy in women? The Beaver Dam Eye Study. *Transactions of the American Ophthalmological Society* 92: 289–297.

Kreijkamp-Kaspers, S., L. Kok, D. E. Grobbee, E. H. de Haan, A. Aleman, J. W. Lampe, and Y. T. van der Schouw. 2004. Effect of soy protein containing isoflavones on cognitive function, bone mineral density, and plasma lipids in postmenopausal women: A randomized controlled trial. *Journal of the American Medical Association* 292: 65–74.

Kronenberg, F., B. Mallory, and J. A. Downey. 1993. Women's health: New frontiers in rehabilitation medicine. *Archives of Physical Medicine and Rehabilitation* 74(12): 1377–1378.

Kuebli, J., and R. Fivush. 1992. Gender differences in parent-child conversations about past emotions. *Sex Roles* 27: 683–698.

Kuhl, H. 2005. Breast cancer risk in the WHI study: The problem of obesity. *Maturitas* 51(1): 83–97.

Kumar, A., W. Bilker, H. Lavretsky, and G. Gottlieb. 2000. Volumetric asymmetries in late-onset mood disorders: An attenuation of frontal asymmetry with depression severity. *Psychiatry Research Neuroimaging* 100: 41–47.

Kumar, A., A. Jin, W. Bilker, J. Udupa, and G. Gottlieb. 1998. Late-onset minor and major depression: Early evidence for common neuroanatomical substrates detected by using MRI. *Proceedings of the National Academy of Science, USA* 95: 7654–7658.

Landen, M., and E. Eriksson. 2003. How does premenstrual dysphoric disorder relate to depression and anxiety disorders? *Depression and Anxiety* 17: 122–129.

Le Blanc, E. S., J. Janowsky, B. K. S. Chan, and H. D. Nelson. 2001. Hormone replacement therapy and cognition: Systematic review and meta-analysis. *Journal of the American Medical Association* 285: 1489–1499.

Lee, S. J., and B. S. McEwen. 2001. Neurotrophic and neuroprotective actions of estrogens and their therapeutic implications. *Annual Review of Pharmacology and Toxicology* 41: 569–591.

Low, L.-F., and K. J. Anstey. 2006. Hormone replacement therapy and cognitive performance in postmenopausal women—A review by cognitive domain. *Neuroscience and Biobehavioral Reviews* 30: 66–84.

Machens, K., and K. Schmidt-Gollwitzer. 2003. Issues to debate on the Women's Health Initiative (WHI) study. Hormone replacement therapy: An epidemiological dilemma? *Human Reproduction* 18(10): 1992–1999.

Mahady, G. B. 2005. Black cohosh (*Actaea/Cimicifuga racemosa*): Review of the clinical data for safety and efficacy in menopausal symptoms. *Treatments in Endocrinology* 4(3): 177–184.

Maki, P. M., and S. M. Resnick. 2001. Effects of estrogen on patterns of brain activity at rest and during cognitive activity: A review of neuroimaging studies. *NeuroImage* 14: 789–801.

Maki, P. M., A. Zonderman, and S. M. Resnick. 2001. Enhanced verbal memory in nondemented elderly women receiving hormone-replacement therapy. *American Journal of Psychiatry* 158: 227–233.

Marcus, S. M., E. A. Young, K. B. Kerber, S. Kornstein, A. H. Farabaugh, J. Mitchell, S. R. Wisniewski, G. K. Balasubramani, M. H. Trivedi, and A. J. Rush. 2005. Gender differences in depression: Findings from the STAR*D study. *Journal of Affective Disorders* 87: 141–150.

Martin, A., and D. J. Cohen. 2000. Adolescent depression: Window of (missed?) opportunity. *American Journal of Psychiatry* 157(10): 1549–1551.

Mazure, C. M., G. P. Keita, and M. C. Blehar. 2002. *Summit on Women and Depression: Proceedings and Recommendations.* American Psychological Association, Washington, DC (October 5–7, 2000).

McEwen, B. S. 2001. Estrogens effects on the brain: Multiple sites and molecular mechanisms (invited review). *Journal of Applied Physiology* 91(6): 2785–2801.

McIntyre, R. S., and K. Fulton. 2005. Letters to the editors: Antidepressant augmentation with raloxifene. *Journal of Clinical Psychopharmacology* 25(1): 96–98.

Metcalf, M. G., and J. H. Livesey. 1995. Distribution of positive moods in women with the premenstrual syndrome and in normal women. *Journal of Psychosomatic Research* 39(5): 609–618.

Miller, K. J. 2003. The other side of estrogen replacement therapy: Outcome study results of mood improvement in estrogen users and nonusers. *Current Psychiatry Reports* 5: 439–444.

Miller, K. J., J. C. Conney, N. L. Rasgon, L. A. Fairbanks, and G. W. Small. 2002. Mood symptoms and cognitive performance in women estrogen users and nonusers and men. *Journal of the American Geriatrics Society* 50: 1826–1830.

Miller, K. J., C. Genest, C. Kernan, P. Siddarth, L. Ercoli, and G. W. Small. 2004. Cognitive profile during perimenopause: Parallels to post-menopause? *Archives of Clinical Neuropsychology* 19(7): 977.

Miller, K. J., and S. A. Rogers. 2005. Depression in women: A closer look at the role of estrogen. In *Mood State and Health*, edited by A. V. Clark, 35–57. Hauppauge, NY: Nova Science Publishers, Inc.

Mitchell, E. S., N. F. Woods, and A. Mariella. 2000. Three stages of the menopausal transition from the Seattle Midlife Women's Health Study: Toward a more precise definition. *Menopause: The Journal of the North American Menopause Society* 75: 334–349.

Mix, J. A., and W. D. Crews Jr. 2002. A double-blind, placebo-controlled, randomized trial of Ginkgo biloba extract EGb 761 in a sample of cognitively intact older adults: Neuropsychological findings. *Human Psychopharmacology* 17(6): 267–277.

Mom, C. H., C. Buijs, P. H. Willemse, M. J. Mourits, and E. G. de Vries. 2006. Hot flushes in breast cancer patients. *Critical Reviews in Oncology/Hematology* 57: 63–77.

Morrison, M. F., M. J. Kallan, T. Ten Have, I. Katz, K. Tweedy, and M. Battistini. 2004. Lack of efficacy of estradiol for depression in postmenopausal women: A randomized, controlled trial. *Biological Psychiatry* 55(4): 406–412.

Mortola, J. F., L. Girton, and U. Fischer. 1991. Successful treatment of severe premenstrual syndrome by combined use of gonadotropin-releasing hormone agonist and estrogen/progestin. *Journal of Clinical Endocrinology and Metabolism* 72(2): 252A–252F.

Nedstrand, E., K. Wijma, Y. Wyon, and M. Hammar. 2005a. Applied relaxation and oral estradiol treatment of vasomotor symptoms in postmenopausal women. *Maturitas* 51(2): 154–162.

———. 2005b. Vasomotor symptoms decrease in women with breast cancer randomized to treatment with applied relaxation or electro-acupuncture: A preliminary study. *Climacteric* 8(3): 243–250.

Nelson, H. D., L. L. Humphrey, P. Nygren, S. M. Teutsch, and J. D. Allan. 2002. Postmenopausal hormone replacement therapy: Scientific review. *Journal of the American Medical Association* 288: 872–881.

Novaes, C., O. P. Almeida, and N. R. de Melo. 1998. Mental health among perimenopausal women attending a menopause clinic: Possible association with premenstrual syndrome? *Climacteric* 1(4): 264–270.

O'Connell, E. 2005. Mood, energy, cognition, and physical complaints: A mind/body approach to symptom management during the climacteric. *Journal of Obstetric, Gynecological, and Neonatal Nursing* 34: 274–279.

Ohkura, T., T. Yasuaki, I. Kunihiro, M. Hiroshi, I. Teruo, S. Yoshihiko, I. Naoya, and Y. Yoshimasa. 1995. Estrogen increases cerebral and cerebellar blood flows in postmenopausal women. *Menopause: Journal of the North American Menopause Society* 2: 13–18.

Paganini-Hill, A., and L. J. Clark. 2000. Preliminary assessment of cognitive function in breast cancer patients treated with tamoxifen. *Breast Cancer Research Treatment* 64: 165–176.

Palinkas, L. A., and E. Barrett-Conner. 1992. Estrogen use and depressive symptoms in postmenopausal women. *Obstetrics and Gynecology* 80: 30–36.

Parker, G. B., and H. L. Brotchie. 2004. From diathesis to dimorphism: The biology of gender differences in depression. *Journal of Nervous and Mental Disease* 192(3): 210–216.

Parry, B. L., C. J. Meliska, L. F. Martinez, N. Basavaraj, G. G. Zirpoli, D. Sorensor, E. L. Maurer, A. Lopez, K. Markova, A. Gamst, T. Wolfson, R. Hauger, and D. F. Kripke. 2004. Menopause: Neuroendocrine changes and hormone replacement therapy. *Journal of the American Medical Women's Association* 59(2): 135–145.

Parry, B. L., and R. P. Newton. 2001. Chronobiological basis of female-specific mood disorders. *Neuropsychopharmacology* 25: S102–S108.

Payne, J. L. 2003. The role of estrogen in mood disorders in women. *International Review of Psychiatry* 15: 280–290.

Pearce, J., K. Hawton, and F. Blake. 1995. Psychological and sexual symptoms associated with the menopause and the effects of hormone replacement therapy. *British Journal of Psychiatry* 167: 163–173.

Pearlstein, T., K. Rosen, and A. B. Stone. 1997. Mood disorders and menopause. *Endocrinology and Metabolism Clinics of North America* 26: 279–294.

Phillips, S. M., and B. B. Sherwin. 1992. Effects of estrogen on memory function in surgically menopausal women. *Psychoneuroendocrinology* 17(5): 485–495.

Piccinelli, M., and G. Wilkinson. 2000. Gender differences in depression. Critical review. *British Journal of Psychiatry* 177: 486–492.

Polo-Kantola, P., R. Erkkola, H. Helenius, K. Irjala, and O. Polo. 1998. When does estrogen replacement therapy improve sleep quality? *American Journal of Obstetrics and Gynecology* 178(5): 1002–1009.

Rapkin, A. 2003. A review of treatment of premenstrual syndrome and premenstrual dysphoric disorder. *Psychoneuroendocrinology* 28: 39–53.

Rasgon, N. L., D. Silverman, P. Siddarth, K. Miller, L. M. Ercoli, S. Elman, H. Lavretsky, S.-C. Huang, M. E. Phelps, and G. W. Small. 2005. Estrogen use and brain metabolic change in postmenopausal women. *Neurobiology of Aging* 26(2): 229–235.

Rasgon, N. L., G. W. Small, P. Siddarth, K. J. Miller, L. M. Ercoli, S. Y. Bookheimer, H. Lavretsky, S. C. Huang, J. R. Barrio, and M. E. Phelps. 2001. Estrogen use and brain metabolic change in older adults. *Psychiatry Research: Neuroimaging Section* 107: 11–18.

Resnick, S. M., P. M. Maki, S. Golski, M. A. Kraut, and A. B. Zonderman. 1998. Effects of estrogen replacement therapy on PET cerebral blood flow and neuropsychological performance. *Hormones and Behavior* 34: 171–182.

Rice, M., A. Graves, and E. Larson. 1995. Estrogen replacement therapy and cognition: Role of phytoestrogens. *Gerontologist* 35(suppl. 1): 169.

Ross, L. E., and M. Steiner. 2003. A biopsychosocial approach to premenstrual dysphoric disorder. *Psychiatric Clinics of North America* 26: 529–546.

Rossano, G. M., C. Vitale, A. Silvestri, and M. Fini. 2003. Hormone replacement therapy and cardioprotection: The end of the tale? *Annals of the New York Academy of Sciences* 997: 351–357.

Rossouw, J. E., G. L. Anderson, R. L. Prentice, A. Z. LaCroix, C. Kooperberg, M. L. Stefanick, R. D. Jackson, S. A. Beresford, B. V. Howard, K. C. Johnson, J. M. Kotchen, and J. Ockene (Writing Group for the Women's Health Initiative Investigators). 2002. Risks and benefits of estrogen plus progestin in healthy postmenopausal women: Principal results from the Women's Health Initiative randomized controlled trial. *Journal of the American Medical Association* 288: 321–323.

Santoro, N., J. Torrens, S. Crawford, J. E. Allsworth, J. S. Finkelstein, E. B. Gold, S. Korenman, W. L. Lasley, J. L. Luborsky, D. McConnell, M. F. Sowers, and G. Weiss. 2005. Correlates of circulating androgens in mid-life women: The study of women's health across the nation. *Journal of Clinical Endocrinology and Metabolism* 90(8): 4836–4845.

Schechter, D. 1999. Estrogen, progesterone, and mood. *Journal of Gender-Specific Medicine* 2(1): 29–36.

Schmidt, P. J., L. K. Nieman, M. A. Danaceau, L. F. Adams, and D. R. Rubinow. 1998. Differential behavioral effects of gonadal steroids in women with and in those without premenstrual syndrome. *New England Journal of Medicine* 338(4): 209–216.

Schneider, L. S., G. W. Small, and C. Clary. 2001. Estrogen replacement therapy and antidepressant response to sertraline in older depressed women. *American Journal of Geriatric Psychiatry* 9: 393–399.

Schneider, L. S., G. W. Small, and the Fluoxetine Collaborative Study Group. 1997. Estrogen replacement and response to fluoxetine in a multicenter geriatric depression trial. *American Journal of Geriatric Psychiatry* 5: 97–106.

Seelig, M. S., B. M. Altura, and B. T. Altura. 2004. Benefits and risks of sex hormone replacement in postmenopausal women. *Journal of the American College of Nutrition* 23(5): 482S–496S.

Sherwin, B. B. 1988. Affective changes with estrogen and androgen replacement therapy in surgically menopausal women. *Journal of Affective Disorders* 14: 177–187.

———. 1990. Estrogen and cognitive functioning in surgically menopausal women. *Psychoneuroendocrinology* 17: 485–495.

———. 1994a. Estrogenic effects on memory in women. *Annals of the New York Academy of Sciences* 743: 213–230.

———. 1994b. No adverse effects of medroxyprogesterone treatment without estrogen in postmenopausal women: Double-blind, placebo-controlled, crossover trial. *Obstetrics and Gynecology* 83(5, part 1): 798–799.

———. 1994c. Sex hormones and psychological functioning in postmenopausal women. *Experimental Gerontology* 29(3–4): 423–430.

————. 1998. Estrogen and cognitive functioning in women. *Proceedings of the Society for Experimental Biology and Medicine* 217: 17–22.

————. 2003. Estrogen and cognitive functioning in women. *Endocrine Reviews* 24(2): 133–151.

Shin, K., and C. Shapiro. 2003. Menopause, sex hormones, and sleep. *Bipolar Disorders* 5: 106–109.

Shoupe, D. 1999. Rationale for ovarian conservation in women. *Menopausal Medicine* 7(3): 1–8.

Silverstein, B. 2002. Gender differences in the prevalence of somatic versus pure depression: A replication. *American Journal of Psychiatry* 159: 1051–1052.

Small, G. W. 1998. Estrogen effects on the brain. *Journal for Gender-Specific Medicine* 1(2): 23–27.

————. 2002. *The Memory Bible: An Innovative Strategy for Keeping Your Brain Young.* New York: Hyperion.

————. contributing editor and Geriatric Psychiatry section editor. 2005. In Kaplan and Sadock's *Comprehensive Textbook of Psychiatry*, 8th ed., edited by B. J. Sadock and V. A. Sadock. Baltimore: Williams & Wilkins.

Small, G. W., and G. Vorgan. 2004. *The Memory Prescription: Dr. Gary Small's 14-Day Plan to Keep Your Brain and Body Young.* New York: Hyperion.

————. 2006. *The Longevity Bible.* New York: Hyperion.

Soares, C. N., and L. S. Cohen. 2001. The perimenopause, depressive disorders, and hormonal variability. *São Paulo Medical Journal* 119(2): 78–83.

Soares, C. N., J. R. Poitras, and J. Prouty. 2003. Effect of reproductive hormones and selective estrogen receptor modulators on mood during menopause. *CNS Drugs* 20(2): 85–100.

Somers, S. 2004. *The Sexy Years.* New York: Random House.

Spinelli, M. G. 2005. Neuroendocrine effects on mood. *Reviews in Endocrine and Metabolic Disorders* 6: 109–115.

Stearns, V. 2006. Serotonergic agents as an alternative to hormonal therapy for the treatment of menopausal vasomotor symptoms. *Treatments in Endocrinology* 5(2): 83–87.

Steiner, M., E. Dunn, and L. Born. 2003. Hormones and mood: From menarche to menopause and beyond. *Journal of Affective Disorders* 74(1): 67–83.

Steiner, M., S. Steinberg, D. Stewart, D. Carter, C. Berger, R. Reid, D. Grover, and D. Streiner, for the Canadian Fluoxetine/Premenstrual Dysphoria Collaborative Study Group. 1995. Fluoxetine in the treatment of premenstrual dysphoria. *New England Journal of Medicine* 332(23): 1529–1534.

Stevens, M. C., V. P. Clark, and K. M. Prestwood. 2005. Low-dose estradiol alters brain activity. *Psychiatry Research* 139(3): 199–217.

Stocky, A., and J. Lynch. 2000. Acute psychiatric disturbance in pregnancy and the puerperium. *Bailliere's Clinical Obstetrics and Gynaecology* 14(1): 73–87.

Studd, J., and N. Panay. 2004. Hormones and depression in women. *Climacteric* 7: 338–346.

Ullman, D. 1991. *Discovering Homeopathic Medicine for the 21st Century*. Berkeley, CA: North Atlantic Books.

van der Schouw, Y. T., and D. E. Grobbee. 2005. Menopausal complaints, oestrogens, and heart disease risk: An explanation for discrepant findings on the benefits of post-menopausal hormone therapy. *European Heart Journal* 26: 1358–1361.

van Dongen, M. C., E. van Rossum, A. G. Kessels, H. J. Sielhorst, and P. G. Knipschild. 2000. The efficacy of ginkgo for elderly people with dementia and age-associated memory impairment: New results of a randomized clinical trial. *Journal of the American Geriatrics Society* 48(10): 1183–1194.

Vassilopoulou-Sellin, R. 2003. Breast cancer and hormonal replacement therapy. *Annals of the New York Academy of Sciences* 997: 341–350.

Villaverde-Gutierrez, C., E. Araujo, F. Cruz, J. M. Roa, W. Barbosa, and G. Ruiz-Villaverde. 2006. Quality of life of rural menopausal women in response to a customized exercise programme. *Journal of Advanced Nursing* 54(1): 11–19.

Vincent, C. A. 1989. A controlled trial of the treatment of migraine by acupuncture. *Clinical Journal of Pain* 5(4): 305–312.

———. 1990. The treatment of tension headache by acupuncture: A controlled single case design with time series analysis. *Journal of Psychosomatic Research* 34(5): 553–561.

Vingerling, J. R., I. Dielemans, J. C. M. Witteman, A. Hofman, D. E. Grobbee, and P. T. V. M. de Jong. 1995. Macular degeneration and early menopause: A case-control study. *British Medical Journal* 310(6994): 1570–1572.

Wallace, O. B., K. S. Lauwers, J. A. Dodge, S. A. May, J. R. Calvin, R. Hinklin, H. U. Bryant, P. K. Shetler, M. D. Adrian, A. G. Geiser, M. Sato, and T. P. Burris. 2006. A selective estrogen receptor modulator for the treatment of hot flashes. *Journal of Medicinal Chemistry* 49(3): 843–846.

Wang, S. J., J. L. Fuh, S. R. Lu, K. D. Juang, and P. H. Wang. 2003. Migraine prevalence during menopausal transition. *Headache* 43(5): 470–478.

Warnock, J. K., J. C. Bundren, and D. W. Morris. 1998. Depressive symptoms associated with gonadotropin-releasing hormone agonists. *Depression and Anxiety* 7: 171–177.

Wassertheil-Smoller, S., S. Shumaker, J. Ockene, G. A. Talavera, P. Greenland, B. Cochrane, J. Robbins, A. Aragaki, and J. Dunbar-Jacob. 2004. Depression and cardiovascular sequelae in postmenopausal women. The Women's Health Initiative (WHI). *Archives of Internal Medicine* 164(3): 289–298.

Wesnes, K. A., T. Ward, A. McGinty, and O. Petrini. 2000. The memory enhancing effects of a Ginkgo biloba/Panax ginseng combination in healthy middle-aged volunteers. *Psychopharmacology (Berlin, Germany)* 152(4): 353–361.

WHI (The Women's Health Initiative Steering Committee). 2004. Effects of conjugated equine estrogen in postmenopausal women with hysterectomy. *Journal of the American Medical Association* 291: 1701–1712.

WHO (World Health Organization Scientific Group). 1981. *Research on the Menopause*. World Health Organization, WHO Technical Services Report Series 670, Geneva, Switzerland (December 8–12, 1980).

Widholm, O., and R. L. Kantero. 1971. A statistical analysis of the menstrual patterns of 8,000 Finnish girls and their mothers. *Acta Obstetricia et Gynecologica Scandinavica Supplement* 14(suppl. 14): 1–36.

Wieck, A. 1996. Ovarian hormones, mood and neurotransmitters. *International Review of Psychiatry* 8(1): 17–25.

Williams, J. E., and D. L. Best. 1982. *Measuring Sex-Stereotypes: A Thirty-Nation Study.* Beverly Hills, CA: Sage.

Wing, R. R., R. W. Jeffery, L. R. Burton, C. Thorson, L. H. Kuller, and A. R. Folsom. 1992. Change in waist-hip ratio with weight loss and its association with change in cardiovascular risk factors. *American Journal of Clinical Nutrition* 55: 1086–1092.

Wing, R. R., K. A. Matthews, L. H. Kuller, E. N. Meilahn, and P. L. Plantinga. 1991. Weight gain at the time of menopause. *Archives of Internal Medicine* 151(1): 97–102.

Wolf, O. T., B. M. Kudielka, D. H. Hellhammer, S. Torber, B. S. McEwen, and C. Kirschbaum. 1999. Two weeks of transdermal estradiol treatment in postmenopausal elderly women and its effect on memory and mood: Verbal memory changes are associated with the treatment induced estradiol levels. *Psychoneuroendocrinology* 24: 727–741.

Wood, R. J., J. S. Volek, S. R. Davis, C. Dell'ova, and M. L. Fernandez. 2006. Effects of a carbohydrate-restricted diet on emerging plasma markers for cardiovascular disease. *Nutrition and Metabolism* 3(1): 19.

Woods, N. F., and E. S. Mitchell. 1997. Pathways to depressed mood for midlife women: Observations from the Seattle Midlife Women's Health Study. *Research in Nursing and Health* 20: 119–129.

———. 2004. Perimenopause: An update. *Nursing Clinics of North America* 39(1): 117–129.

Woolley, C. S. 1999. Effects of estrogen in the CNS. *Current Opinion in Neurobiology* 9: 349–354.

Wyon, Y., R. Lindgren, T. Lundeberg, and M. Hammar. 1995. Effects of acupuncture on climacteric vasomotor symptoms, quality of life, and urinary excretion of neuropeptides among postmenopausal women. *Menopause: Journal of the North American Menopause Society* 2(1): 3–12.

Yaffe, K., K. Krueger, S. R. Cummings, T. Blackwell, V. W. Henderson, S. Sarkar, K. Ensrud, and D. Grady. 2005. Effect of raloxifene on prevention of dementia and cognitive impairment in older women: The Multiple Outcomes of Raloxifene Evaluation (MORE) randomized trial. *American Journal of Psychiatry* 162(4): 683–690.

Yaffe, K., K. Krueger, S. Sarkar, D. Grady, E. Barrett-Connor, D. A. Cox, and T. Nickelsen (for the Multiple Outcomes of Raloxifene Evaluation investigators). 2001. Cognitive function in postmenopausal women treated with raloxifene. *New England Journal of Medicine* 344(16): 1242–1244.

Young, E. A., and M. Altemus. 2004. Puberty, ovarian steroids, and stress. *Annals of the New York Academy of Sciences* 1021: 124–133.

Young, E. A., and A. Korszun. 2002. The hypothalamic-pituitary-gonadal axis in mood disorders. *Endocrinology and Metabolism Clinics of North America* 31: 63–78.

Zec, R. F., and M. A. Trivedi. 2002. The effects of estrogen replacement therapy on neuropsychological functioning in postmenopausal women with and without dementia: A critical and theoretical review. *Neuropsychology Review* 12: 65–109.

Zhao, L., K. O'Neill, and R. D. Brinton. 2005. Selective estrogen receptor modulators (SERMs) for the brain: Current status and remaining challenges for developing NeuroSERMs. *Brain Research Reviews* 49: 472–493.

Zweifel, J. E., and W. H. O'Brien. 1997. A meta-analysis of the effect of hormone replacement therapy upon depressed mood. *Psychoneuroendocrinology* 22(3): 189–212.

Marti Olsen Laney, Psy.D., MFT, is a psychotherapist, researcher, author, consultant, and lively public speaker. Her first book, *The Introvert Advantage: How to Thrive in an Extrovert World*, has become nationally recognized as *the* book on introversion and has been translated into fifteen languages. Her second book, *The Hidden Gifts of the Introverted Child: Helping your Child Thrive in an Extroverted World*, has been widely acclaimed by school counselors, therapists, and parents. Marti has appered on more than two-hundred radio and television programs in America and Canada. Marti, an introvert, has been married for forty-two years to her extrovert husband, Michael.

Michael L. Laney, MBA, CPA, is a busines consultant providing organizational development, strategic planning, and advisory board-of-director services. He is certified in the Myers-Briggs Type Indicator (MBTI). He has consulted with his wife, Marti, on her book projects and was the "roadie" on each of her book tours. He has appearesd on several radio and television shows with his Marti to discuss the ins and outs of their introvert-extrovert relationship.